MAINE'S COASTAL
CEMETERIES
A Historic Tour

Maine's Coastal CEMETERIES
A Historic Tour

By
Karen Wentworth Batignani

Printed and bound at Versa Press, Inc., East Peoria, IL.

5   4   3   2   1

Down East Books
Camden, ME
Book Orders: 800-685-7962
www.downeastbooks.com
A division of Down East Enterprise,
publishers of *Down East* magazine
www.downeast.com

Library of Congress Control Number: 2003107249

Acknowledgments

To Michael and Alison I extend my deep gratitude and love for your constant faith in all of my endeavors, no matter how curious.

This book would not be possible without the research of those who were and are dedicated to preserving their town histories. The following historical societies shared their resources: Kittery Historic and Naval Museum, Old Berwick Historical Society, York Village Historical Society, Maine Historical Society, Yarmouth Historical Society, Freeport Historical Society, Brunswick Historical Society, Gray Historical Society, Harpswell Historical Society, Waldoboro Historical Society, Warren Historical Society, Monhegan Historical and Cultural Museum, Vinalhaven Historical Society, Belfast Historical Society, Castine Historical Society, Blue Hill Historical Society, Machias Historical Society, and Eastport Historical Society.

This project has deepened my appreciation of our public libraries and for librarians, whose knowledge and expertise is a marvel.

I am especially thankful to those people who took me on tours of cemeteries, and to those who graciously shared their time, knowledge and resources. Norma Keim, Wendy Pirsig, James Kences, Brother Paul Bolduc, William Tate, William Jordan, Harriet Price, Barbara Desmarais, David Hackett, Gary Best, Margery Freeman, Dick Ferrin, Tralice Bracy, Beth Eddy of the Rockland Cemetery Association, Valerie Morton, Megan Pinette, Douglas Coffin, Bradford Tenney of the Castine Cemetery Association, Sally Foote, Elvera Bass, Valdeen Atwood, Mike Kimball, Francis Ray, Terry Holt, Arther Speiss of the Maine Historical Preservation Commission and John Spauding of the Association for Gravestone Studies.

Karen Wentworth Batignani

Table of Contents

Introduction

Did you know that in the mid-1800s some cemeteries printed postcards, provided tours, and were listed in guidebooks as major attractions? The artistically landscaped cemeteries that appeared between 1831 and 1860 were celebrated tourist destinations that attracted thousands of American and European visitors. Cemeteries were viewed as peaceful meditative places where it was possible to escape from the anxieties of the everyday world. People flocked to them expecting to learn spiritual lessons from the epitaphs, consider their mortality, acknowledge history, and honor the dead. Women were encouraged to bring their children to acquaint them with death, foster compassion, and inspire them with the ambitious deeds of those who had come before.

Gradually, after the 1860s, the appeal of cemeteries subsided, and Americans grew less comfortable with cemeteries and death. But recently, interest is being renewed. Cemetery preservation groups are growing in number. Schools are taking children on field trips to the local graveyard to learn about the first settlers. Historical societies are busy researching and documenting their early graveyards.

When I disclose that I love old cemeteries, people generally react in one of two ways. Some people become uncomfortable, may awkwardly giggle or make a reference to morbidness. But more often people will quietly confess that they, too, love cemeteries and will frequently tell me of their favorite. Their reasons vary: genealogy, seeking the graves of the famous, finding veterans, grave rubbing, a love of history, or simply for quiet walks. Personally, I am a kindred spirit with the tourist of the 19th century. I find them to be sacred contemplative places that calm my spirit. By remembering death, I am reminded to live fully. As I read the gravestone inscriptions, I am inspired by the accomplishments and moved to tears by the tragedies. And always my imagination is activated—What were their lives like?

On these pages, I offer thirty-eight of my favorite Maine coast cemeteries. The criterion used for choosing from the hundreds along the coast was a subjective process. Features that influenced me included a rich history, well-carved stones, a variety of stones, notable people, stunning water views, park-like grounds, woodland settings, location, and those indefinable qualities that create personality and ambience. Few cemeteries were too small or too old, but I avoided the new and the large. Most often I was directed to the best cemeteries by the wonderful people who staff libraries and historical societies, and are so willing to share their time and knowledge. Sometimes serendipitous conversations or bits of information led me to great finds.

The amount of history provided for each chapter was determined by availability. When chapters are large it is because I had the good fortune of having a guide walk me through the cemetery and graciously supply historical data they had compiled, or the local historical society or library had well-researched, organized material that was readily available. This book is not a scholarly attempt at history, so I've included oral traditions, folklore and speculation and always to the best of my knowledge labeled it as such.

While researching individuals it became evident that there are many people missing from our historical records. Information about women, African Americans, Native Americans and the poor is hard to come by. I have made an effort to include whatever was available. Also, it is important to remember that even though this book has several stories of death at the hands of Native Americans, far more Native Americans were killed than those of European descent.

I would like to share a helpful observation. During the glorious summer months that I've traveled coastal Maine hunting for cemeteries, I came to understand that they truly are the best tourist destinations. There is never a problem with parking, there are no lines, it is always quiet, and the views are great. Be sure to bring a lawn chair!

Cemeteries and Gravestones:
A PRIMER

The early settlers did not have the luxury of cemeteries. Most families buried their dead in a high spot on their property. Gravestones were not available until after 1660, or even later in rural settlements, so wooden slabs or crosses and fieldstones were used to mark graves. Harsh weather, long distances, and personal preference were factors in some families'continued use of their burial ground even after their town or church created cemeteries. As you drive along Maine's roads you'll see many small family burial grounds that date well into the 1800s, or even to the present. After a settlement was established, building a meetinghouse or church was one of the first priorities. The settlers followed the English tradition of the churchyard cemetery. The Old Common Cemetery in Harpswell and the German Protestant Cemetery in Waldoboro are outstanding examples as their meeting-houses have had few renovations. When a town cemetery was established early, then it was generally in the center of the village, such as the Ancient Cemetery in Wiscasset. In Portland, Eastern Cemetery, with burials dating back to the 17th century, takes up six acres of city land. In the older graveyards, not much thought was given to planning or appearance, and often graves are haphazard. Sometimes town cemeteries started as family burial grounds and the town bought the surrounding acreage. In other instances a group of businessmen formed a cemetery, as in the John Carver Cemetery in Vinalhaven.

After the 1830s, cemetery design changed radically. Concerns about disease and odor pushed cemeteries out of city centers and churchyards. In Cambridge, Massachusetts, Mount Auburn Cemetery opened in 1831, and became the inspiration for cemeteries around the country. Mount Auburn mixed gravestones, memorials, tombs, and monuments on 174 acres with roads that curved around ponds, streams, and some of the most stunning landscape design that America had ever seen. Designated as a "rural cemetery" it became a tourist destination that attracted thousands every year. Anytime you enter a 19th-century cemetery with park-like grounds, then Mount Auburn was its inspiration. The Seaside Cemetery in Blue Hill or Glen Cove

Cemetery in Rockland are small cemeteries, but their grounds are well landscaped and aesthetically pleasing.

Headstones, monuments, tombs, and memorials hold deep meaning as they reflect attitudes about life and death. The inscriptions tell of the values, virtues, religious beliefs, accomplishments, and tragedies of those who lie below. The motifs carved on gravestones are the symbols of our unconscious or perhaps the collective unconscious. Like art, cemeteries and grave markers are subject to the vagaries of fashion, with styles that come and go, reflecting the culture of the times.

Many scholars have studied grave markers and created timelines that are guides for dating stones and understanding the period in which they originated. The timelines are important for understanding graveyards, but they must also be considered flexible. It is essential to remember that while some places along the Maine coast were quite metropolitan, other places during the same period were still struggling settlements in the wilderness. York Village's oldest gravestone is dated 1705 and is carved with the winged death head typical of the times. But in many small settlements farther north, a carved gravestone may not have made an appearance until after 1763, when the French and Indian Wars

The winged death head was common on 18th-century gravestones.

ended. The following is a brief overview of the established timelines for gravestone styles, but keep in mind that they are generalities and there are always exceptions.

The oldest gravestones found on this tour date from the early 1700s, with the winged death head on dark slate being the most common period symbol. A skull with crossbones, symbolizing mortal remains, is occasionally found. Symbolically, the addition of wings to the skull joins the mortal remains with the soul's heavenward journey. The stern winged death heads are frightening in their countenance and remind us that the early Congregationalists believed that few were chosen for salvation and many were predestined to damnation. Original sin, an active Devil, fear, and guilt were their religious companions. Besides death heads, stone cutters also used skeletons, hourglasses, and coffins—carvings that carefully avoided any overt religious significance that could be associated with Catholic idolatry. Epitaphs were not written as memories to the deceased, but as warnings to the living that they, too, would die and must prepare for it.

During the 1730s a series of religious revivals brought on the Great Awakening, with its teachings that God was kind and forgiving. Views of death became more optimistic. The death head gave way to the winged cherub, also called the winged soul. Sometimes the face of the deceased was winged. The winged cherub symbolized the soul's journey to the afterlife and reflects a softened attitude towards God and death. Warnings of death in epitaphs were replaced with eager longing for release from the harshness of life. Slate was still the most commonly used stone, and there was more variety incorporated in the designs, with grapes, vines, flowers, rosettes, hearts, heavenly bodies, and horns employed.

Several influences brought about a rapid change in gravestone carvings in the years following the Revolutionary War. The Federalist Period, from 1790 to 1820, saw a keen interest in ancient Roman and Greek democracy. Americans turned away from England's influence and favored Neoclassical art and Greek Revival architecture, which was inspired by the 18th-century excavations in Pompeii and Herculaneum. During the same period Unitarian and Universalist Churches, along with the spirit of the Enlightenment, encouraged secularism. On gravestones this resulted in the nearly total dominance of the willow and urn motif in many places by 1805 and almost everywhere along the coast by the 1830s. Sometimes the willow and urn are depicted singularly, but most often they are together. The urns of ancient Greece and the clean lines of Neoclassicism influenced the designs. There is little variety, though by the 1830s marble replaced slate as the favored stone.

The urn had long been a symbol for the death of the flesh or as a receptacle for human remains. The use of the willow tree, symbolizing earthly sorrow, probably originated from Psalm 137:1-2,

The willow and urn motif, like this one from a gravestone in Wiscasset, had become very popular by the 1830s.

which states, "By the rivers of Babylon, there we sat down, yea we wept, when we remembered Zion. We hanged up our harps upon the willows in the midst thereof." The combination of the willow and urn symbolizes grief over mortal loss.

After the 1830s, the design and intent of cemeteries changed drastically. The movement towards integrating nature and landscape with grave markers resulted in the use of statues, obelisks, columns, and monuments by those who could afford them. Slate disappeared and was replaced by marble that, in many instances, was unadorned. Of those that were carved, relief sculptures of birds, animals, and flowers reflected the new interest in nature. In mid-century, the Victorian Era took hold in America and grave markers became more elaborate, with beautiful relief motifs and lettering. For the first time children had their own symbols: lambs and angels for innocence. One of the effects of the Industrial Revolution was that the home took on special significance, and on grave markers draperies, columns, books, and rooms appeared. Epitaphs were sentimental and poetic, with death being romanticized.

The 20th-century stones that populate Maine's coastal cemeteries are far less interesting than their predecessors. Polished granite blocks offer names and dates but few clues as to who the deceased were. What are the factors that influenced the anonymous grave markers of our lifetime? A few philosophers speculate that we are a culture in denial about death and point to steel-lined gorgeously cushioned caskets, air-conditioned tombs, and cryonics as proof. Does denial of death, community breakdown, Existentialism or Modernism impact our gravestone choices? What will people say were the influences on us one hundred years from now? There are reasons to hope for a promising trend towards markers that reveal more about the deceased. Sand-blasting techniques are being used to create nature scenes and even portraits. Relatives landscape some gravesites, and the stones act as altars where treasures of rocks, shells, toys, and holiday decorations are offered. Epitaphs seem to be returning, as well as inscriptions telling a bit about the person. Let's hope that the 21st century brings with it a renaissance of interesting grave markers.

Map of Coastal Maine

Route I

Route I

N

Part One

SOUTHERN MAINE

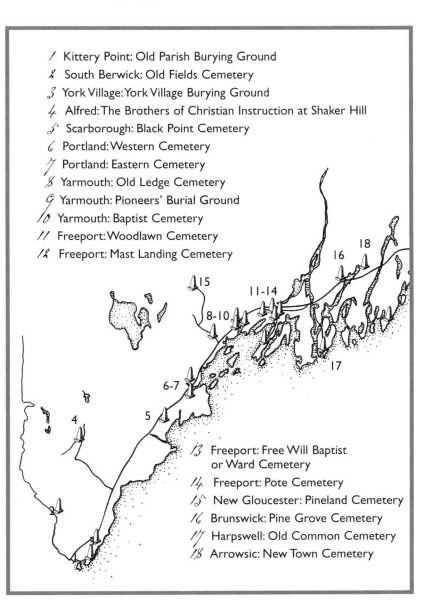

1 Kittery Point: Old Parish Burying Ground

2 South Berwick: Old Fields Cemetery

3 York Village: York Village Burying Ground

4 Alfred: The Brothers of Christian Instruction at Shaker Hill

5 Scarborough: Black Point Cemetery

6 Portland: Western Cemetery

7 Portland: Eastern Cemetery

8 Yarmouth: Old Ledge Cemetery

9 Yarmouth: Pioneers' Burial Ground

10 Yarmouth: Baptist Cemetery

11 Freeport: Woodlawn Cemetery

12 Freeport: Mast Landing Cemetery

13 Freeport: Free Will Baptist or Ward Cemetery

14 Freeport: Pote Cemetery

15 New Gloucester: Pineland Cemetery

16 Brunswick: Pine Grove Cemetery

17 Harpswell: Old Common Cemetery

18 Arrowsic: New Town Cemetery

Kittery Point
OLD PARISH BURYING GROUND

Directions: From Route 1, take Route 236 south to Route 103, Kittery Point. The cemetery is on the right, across from the First Congregational Church.

To fully enjoy the Old Parish Burying Ground in Kittery Point, bring a lawn chair and a picnic lunch. It is one of the prettiest cemeteries in Maine, with its view of the Piscataqua River, an array of flowers and vegetation, secret nooks and crannies, and proximity to the First Congregational Church and Lady Pepperrell House. In this single cemetery, 250 years of gravestone styles can be traced, starting in 1733 and moving through to the present. There are fine samples of early slate stones carved with winged death heads, winged cherubs, crowned angels, willows and urns, and even a ship tossed in a stormy sea. The most prevalent gravestones in the Old Parish Burying Ground are the white marble stones often decorated with the floral designs and religious motifs that dominated graveyards throughout the 19th century. Here you will also find the ubiquitous polished granite blocks that appeared as the 20th century unfolded.

The Robert Browning epitaph written for Levi Lincoln Thaxter has brought the cemetery a degree of fame. Thaxter was a fan of Browning's and the husband of the poet Celia Thaxter. Celia and Levi married when she was 16 and he was 30, and though they never divorced, they led separate

Robert Browning wrote the epitaph for Maine poet Celia Thaxter's husband, Lincoln.

lives. She is buried in her family plot on Appledore in the Isles of Shoals, New Hampshire. Their three sons, Levi, Karl, and Roland are buried here. His stone can be found nestled in a corner towards the right back. The epitaph was originally carved directly onto the boulder, but when this became difficult to read, the epitaph was cast in bronze and bolted over the original carving. It reads:

> Thou, whom these eyes saw never! Say friends true
> Who say my soul, helped onward by my song,
> Thou all unwitting has helped thee too?
> I gave of but the little that I knew:
> How were the gift requited, while along
> Life's path I pace, could thou make weakness strong?
> Help me with knowledge—for Life's Old—Death's New!

Wander down the path under the apple tree to find several slate stones surrounded by an abundance of phlox, daisies, ferns, and beach roses. Here you will find the grave of Margaret Hills.

> Margaret Hills
> consort of
> Oliver Hills
> Died Oct 31st 1803
> Aet. 28
> I lost my life in raging sea's
> A Sov'reign God does as he please
> The Kittery friends they did appear,
> And my remains they buried here.

Traveling back up to the main cemetery, look for a handsome black stone carved with a ship in a tumultuous ocean.

> Brig Hattie Eaton
> W.I. to Boston
> Island Mch 21, 1876
> Crew of 8, white
> And Negro, and 1 stowaway
> Near this stone lie six
> Bodies never claimed

This stunning carving marks the grave of the crew of the ship, Hattie Eaton.

Next to this is a 1759 stone that is an example, though not a particularly good one, of Puritan stone carving. Note how the periods are suspended, and the stylized capital letters are heavily carved.

Along the stockade fence, in a hidden nook that would make a suitable spot for a child's secret fort, is a miniature obelisk surrounded by a delicate wrought-iron fence. It reads:

Charles Frances Hagner
1844
A lamb of the first year without blemish

In the front left you'll find an array of 18th-century headstones featuring winged death heads, some with fearsome teeth; there is also a winged cherub, and an unusual carving of crowned angels.

An unusual carving of a pair of crowned angels.

In many older graveyards you will find this 18th-century classic or some version of it:

Behold all men as you pass by,
As you are now, so once was I:
As I am now, so you must be,
Prepare for death and follow me.

The preceding epitaph is very well known, but the next two are truly unconventional.

Old and Still

and

By my request
Let this dust rest

In the left front is the large table tomb of the Cutts family, with dates ranging from 1795 to 1869. The Cutts were successful ship-builders and a distinguished New England name. Their lengthy epitaph is fascinating as it discloses the events that led to their loss of fortune. Local history tells us that Captain Joseph Cutts "lost his reason" after doing the same with his fortune, while one of his sons "fell by his own hand." But it is the Captain's daughter, Miss Sally Cutts, who fascinates people most as she becomes insane. Miss Sally lived on in the Lady Pepperrell House, which sits perpendicular to the cemetery, long after it decayed into disrepair. Rumors that the house was haunted did not stop kindly people from furnishing her material needs, while she, in her madness, believed that the government was going to return her family's lost money. The author Sarah Orne Jewett, whose home is in South Berwick, wrote of Sally Cutts in her book *Deephaven*.

Across the street from the Old Parish Burying Ground is the state's oldest meetinghouse, the First Congregational Church, organized in 1714 and built in 1730. This meetinghouse, along with others you encounter, has had many renovations over the years, which is a study within itself. Early cemeteries were often planned in proximity to meetinghouses. A community's meetinghouse was not only for services on the Sabbath, it was also the venue for town meetings, as well as a gathering place in times of danger or emergency. It was variously a refuge against Native American attacks, a weapons storehouse, and the site where whipping posts and stocks would appear. In early New England, church and state were not separate, but inseparable.

The Old Parish Burying Ground is one of Maine's outstanding cemeteries, with its rich history spanning 250 years. It combines a beautiful, serene setting and fascinating gravestones. Enjoy.

Also Visit:
The **Kittery Historic and Naval Museum** is a treasure trove of information about this early Maine settlement. Kittery has a

well-documented history, and the museum is very accommodating. Open June through early fall. Tel: (207) 439-3080.

The **Portsmouth Naval Shipyard Museum** exhibits 19th-century shipbuilding memorabilia, artifacts, and models. A large portion of the museum examines 20th-century submarines, and includes several models. Open July and August. Monday through Friday from 10:00 to 4:00. Walker Street, Kittery. Tel: (207) 438-1000.

the characters in Sarah Orne Jewett's novel about the Revolutionary War, *The Tory Lover.*

Hamilton's success was not enjoyed by his children, who lost the family fortune and left the area. The Embargo Act of 1807 and the War of 1812 financially ruined the trading businesses of many merchants and probably precipitated their loss.

Another person admired by the community is buried under the massive oak tree. On a humble Maine boulder is a plaque stating:

> Dr. JBM Gray
> An Oxford honor man who from 1855-1857
> Was preceptor of Berwick Academy
> An inspiring teacher of vast learning
> And greatly beloved.

William Hayes Ward (1835-1916) was honored for his progressive ideas. He was an editor of the *New York Independent,* which was a literary magazine that published "My Butterfly, An Elegy," by Robert Frost. It was Frost's first publication in a national magazine.

> Teacher, Editor
> Friend of the Indian
> Defender of the Negro
> Promotor (sic) of Church Unity
> Orientalist, Poet
> Interpreter of God
> Follower of Christ
> Moreover because the preacher was wise
> He still taught the people knowledge.

According to his epitaph, John Hill was an active and well respected man. Like Hamilton's, Hill's epitaph expounds on his accomplishments and virtues. I refer to these as "virtue epitaphs." They are common in communities where there was enough wealth to afford the large stones and extensive carving. John Hill's stone is a wonderful example of this, but becomes especially interesting when viewed in relation to his wife's. Comparing the two epitaphs tells us volumes about the status of women in the late 18th century. His impressively cut stone states:

In memory
of the Honble (sic)
John Hill esq.
Who after 28 years successfully
Serving the Massachusetts Bay as
a member of his Majesty's Council
resign'd his Seat at the Board:
At the time of his Death, and for
many years before, he sustained
the Offices of first Justice of the
Interior Court and Judge of Probate
for York County
Honesty and integrity
marked his path thro' life
with distinguished luster.
He died the 2d of March 1772

Compare John's with Sarah's for a glimpse at the criteria used to determine a woman's worth.

Mrs. Sarah Hill
wife of late
Hon. John Hill
and late widow of
Rev. John Blunt
and daughter of
Hon. John Frost
of Newcastle. N.H.
Died 1772

There are many hints in Old Fields Cemetery that South Berwick had a sizable number of wealthy residents. There are several large tombs; many well-cut head- and footstones, and carvings that reflect the current trends. In progressive places along the coast, the winged death head and cherub had disappeared by the late 1700s, but in northern or inland communities they can be spotted into the 19th century. In 1799, urns were in vogue, and Fanny Hovey's beautifully lettered gravestone, deeply cut with an urn of original design, was the height of fashion, even if it was amateur in its execution. It is towards the back left. The stone also shows us that the 20th century construct for the stages of grieving developed by Elisabeth Kubler-Ross were very much a part of the human psyche in 1799. Ivory Hovey appears to have been wrestling with denial when this inscription was written.

> Here rests for a season
> Fanny
> Dauth (sic) of Ivory Francis Hovey
> She was born Febry 7th 1779
> And fell asleep May 3d 1799

A moving epitaph continues on in the most loving prose.

Dr. Hovey was a surgeon during the Revolutionary War and prospered afterwards into one of South Berwick's wealthiest men. His good fortune with money did not transfer to other aspects of his life; none of his children survived, and he was widowed twice. Near Fanny's slate is a single stone carved with three small cherubs marking the burials of three infants. His son Temple died in 1811 at the age of 36, and two of Ivory's three wives are here as well. Note that the first

The gravestone of Fanny Hovey features a unique carving of an urn.

two wives were the sisters Mary and Francis Hight. Francis died in 1816, and in 1817 Ivory married Sarah March of Newburyport. After only a year of marriage, Ivory died at the age of 70, and his simple stone is close to the others. After Ivory's death, it became evident that his estate was insolvent. It is believed that Sarah stayed on for a time, living in the best style she could with limited means, and folklore claims that the ghosts of Ivory's first wives ruthlessly haunted her. In Sarah Orne Jewett's short story, "River Driftwood" from *Country By-Ways*, she writes of Ivory Hovey as the handsome and generous physician who lived in a grand style. Her story speaks of the rumor that his first wife was murdered and that his last wife was haunted by both poverty and ghosts.

In the wooded area to the right are the graves of Margaret Fife and her five children, with marble stones in graduating sizes from small to large. Margaret passed on at the age of 41 and her children died between the ages of 14 years and 1 month. Touching epitaphs accompany their stones.

Towards the center right you'll find a headstone engraved, "Mary relict of Capt. Elisha Hill." Relict is an archaic term for a widow. Notice how the winged cherub that adorns her stone has had her mouth scraped and re-carved, probably to redo the lips. Occasionally stones can be found that have been scraped clear and redone, though they are not always as obvious as this one.

Near the back woods rest two members of the Chadbourne family.

> Margaret & Abigail
> Chadbourne
> Jan. 11 1862　　　June 24 1858
> æt. 78　　　　　　æt. 72
> Both
> Friendly in life, happy in Death
> Tribute from surviving friends

Their epitaphs reflect the common theme of the era that death was God's reward for a life well lived.

Among the many special stones here is a zinc marker, tucked along the right-hand edge, which is unique because of its small size. Also, note Captain John Lord's stone towards the rear right. Look carefully at Captain Lord's stone as it is difficult to see the carving because it is so shallow. It is rich in Free Mason symbolism and is a prime example of a popular early 19th-century style.

The lack of maintenance at Old Fields Cemetery has the unintended effect of creating an enchanted woodland setting, but, unfortunately, the neglect reflects poorly on the gravestones that are in dire need of cleaning before their messages are lost. Nevertheless, this is a wonderful place to wile away the hours.

Also of Interest:

virtue epitaph that exalts her best characteristics, but more interesting is the date of death: Jan. 29 1727/8. This is an example of the use of an older-style calendar in which the new year began in March.

Samuel and Hannah Moody's infant daughter's grave is the earliest stone in the cemetery. Lucy's stone is still legible and its diminutive size is touching. A winged death head tops the stone, with "Resurrection" cut beneath. The epitaph reads:

> To immortality in Spotless Beauty
> with all other Bodily Perfection's
> after the fashion of Christ's
> Glorious Body, is expected for
> The sub(?)adjacent Dust
> of Lucy Moody who was born
> and died July the 6 1705
> Thous birth spousals to
> Christ, Death, Coronation
> all in one day may have their
> celebration

On 18th-century gravestones, "spotless beauty" or "bodily perfection" is frequently mentioned when the deceased is an infant or a young child.

The French and Indian War of the late 17th century resulted in the abandonment of many settlements north of Wells. In York, the contentious relationship culminated on January 25, 1692 when a morning attack by the Abenaki resulted in the death of forty colonists and the capture of eighty, who were then herded to Canada, many dying en route. The number of dead and captured has never been verified, but is based on an oral tradition. Seventeen houses were burned, businesses and homes were looted, and lead objects were taken to be melted into bullets. Food products were destroyed to ensure hunger for the rest of the season. A monument memorializes what became known as the Candlemas Day Massacre.

Buried here is Jeremiah Moulton, whose life was forever impacted by the massacre. As a four-year-old, he witnessed the scalping and murder of his parents. He was captured with the intention of bringing him to Canada, but the tiny Jeremiah went into such a rage and reacted with such belligerence that he became a source of amusement to the Abenaki, who teased him a bit and then apparently allowed him to escape. Perhaps it would have served the Abenaki better if they had taken young Jeremiah back with them, for he vowed to avenge the deaths of his parents and, true to his word, became a dedicated "Indian fighter."

Moulton became determined to destroy a large permanent Abenaki settlement that was overseen by the Jesuit priest, Father Sebastian Râle. The English believed that Father Râle, who espoused the French cause, encouraged Native American raids. To the French and Abenaki, Father Râle was a spiritual leader and teacher who wrote an Abenaki dictionary (now at Harvard University), built two churches, and worked to improve the quality of life for the natives. Regardless of where the truth lies, Râle became a target for the English.

Dummer's War, which lasted from 1721 to 1726, was the fourth war in a series of six involving the Abenaki and settlers in Maine. As part of this war, Moulton led a contingent to Norridgewock in 1723. They planned their attack for the dead of winter, hoping to surprise the settlement and capture Râle. Somehow, advance notice had reached Norridgewock and Moulton found a temporarily abandoned village. His next opportunity came the following year, when he was one of the leaders of a two-hundred-man expedition divided into four units. This time the village was destroyed and a large number of men, women, and children were killed. The commanders were under orders to return with the priest alive, but to Moulton's disappointment, Râle was scalped and murdered along with the others. There are two different accounts as to how it occurred. In one report, Râle and others were being held captive, but overnight they were scalped and murdered against orders. In the other account, he was shot many times as Native Americans jumped to shield him.

Norridgewock was decimated and the church burned. The English had believed that by destroying the village they would ensure the safety of the southern settlements because the Abenaki would be too fearful to retaliate. Instead, emotions were further inflamed, and the Abenaki demanded that settlements west of the Saco River be abandoned. The war continued for another two years.

Moulton's gravestone reads:

Jeremiah Moulton
York Soldier in Indian
War 1725
Here lyes Buried the Body
of the

Honbl (sic) Jeremiah Moulton, ESQ
who departed this life
July the 20th 1765
Aged 77 years

The Emerson-Wilcox House backs the burial ground and is a museum. On display inside is the famous wool crewel bedding referred to as the Bulman Bedhangings. Mary Bulman Prentice, who is buried in the graveyard, embroidered them around 1745. Mary lived across the street from the Emerson-Wilcox House and probably began the hangings while her husband, Dr. Alexander Bulman, was with Pepperrell on the campaign to Louisburg. They are the only complete set of American bedhangings and are extraordinary in their detail. It appears that she was well educated, as the valance is embroidered with the poem "Meditation in the Grove," by Isaac Watt.

York's most infamous gravestone is Mary Nasson's. When entering from the parking lot, it can be easily spotted due to the large slab between the headstone and the footstone. The portrait stone is believed to be carved by Joseph Lamson, from the well-known family of Boston stonecutters. In local lore, Mary's grave is referred to as the "witch's grave" because it was believed that the large slab was needed to keep her spirit from rising to haunt the living. Interestingly, the rusticator Elizabeth Perkins, who was one of York's most industrious Colonial Revivalists, invented the legend to inspire tourists to visit York. In reality, Nasson's husband probably placed it there to keep animals from digging it up or to protect it after the family moved to Sanford. A local historian and expert on the cemetery, James Kences, believes that the odd slab was Nasson's attempt to imitate the boxlike monuments, or mock sarcophagi, that was a common English style used by wealthier colonists. It's hard to swallow that anyone could believe Nasson was a witch, considering her lovely portrait and endearing epitaph.

Here rests quite free from Life's
Distressing care
A loving wife
A tender Parent dear
Cut down in midst of Days
As you may see,
But stop my Grief
I soon shall equal be.

When death shall stop
my breath
And end my Time,
God grant my Dust
May mingle then with thine.
Sacred to the Memory of Mary Nasson
wife of Samuel Nasson who departed
this Life August 28 1774
æt at 29

Mrs. Lucy Sewall, who died in 1800 at the age of 43, was also greatly missed, according to her epitaph, which reads like a love letter:

Blessed Shade! Thy life is not
measured by age, nor thy memory
by death: thou still livest on the
tongue of friendship & charity
Thy praise still glows in the heart of
conjugal & filial tenderness. The bosom
of an affectionate husband & the tears
of an orphan shall perpetuate the
remembrance of thee till our
kindred souls unite in those realms
where pain and sorrow never afflict
Thine was the hand on other's wants relieved
And thine the heart to pity ever mov'd

Lucy Sewell's tender epitaph may be due to her untimely passing. As people aged, their epitaphs became less heartfelt and more descriptive of culturally desirable virtues. After dying at the age of 74, in 1761, we learn of Mrs. Hannah Sweet's exceptional character traits. Her epitaph also expresses fascinating imagery.

Her life was an example of Piety
Diligence Frugality & Charity
Her soil now lodged above ye Rolling Spheres
The baleful influence of whose giddy dance
Sheds sad vicissitude on all beneath

In older cemeteries, at least one family can be found who have lost several children; frequently they will all be named on a single cornfields, hayfields, a store, a maple-sugar house, a greenhouse, and a carriage house that is being renovated by the Friends of the Alfred Shaker Museum. There are regular Sunday church services. There are many fine flower gardens and an impressive diversity of plants growing on the grounds. In 1931, 750 kinds of plants were documented on Shaker Hill. The Shakers grew many unusual plants that they used for household and medicinal purposes. Prickly ash, used for quieting toothaches, grows between the barn and the pond, and on "Indigo Hill," indigo still grows profusely.

My guide was Brother Paul Bolduc, who charmed me with his warmth and impressed me with his historic knowledge. Unfortunately, he has passed away. Blessings to you, Brother Bolduc. Open year round. **Tel:** (207) 324-6160 or (888) 306-2271.

The "Old Fire Station" houses the **Alfred Village Museum,** which features changing displays by local organizations as well as permanent exhibits. The permanent historical displays are divided into categories: Firehouse Memories, Town Hall, Sunday Morning, School Days, and Victorian Parlor. Open June through August on Wednesdays and Saturdays from 2:00 to 4:00. In July and August, also open on Mondays. Oak Street, Alfred. For more information call Allison Williams, (207) 324-5823 or Elizabeth Morrison, (207) 324-7650.

BLACK POINT CEMETERY

Directions: From Route 1 in Scarborough, turn onto Route 207, Black Point Road. The cemetery will be 1.5 miles down on the left. Enter at 7th Avenue.

A steady stream of cars zooms past Black Point Cemetery, belying its park-like restful atmosphere. It is fairly large, well kept, and landscaped with oak trees, evergreens and decorative bushes. In the front section of 7th Avenue you will find historic stones that date back to the mid 18th century. There are also many 19th-century markers, but the largest part of the cemetery is given over to the 20th century.

Black Point Cemetery is home to numerous gravestones carved by my favorite stonecutter, Joseph Sikes. His stones are quite adorned for the region, and the mournful heads are poignant reminders of grief.

History offers us scant information about stonecutters. Often they were masons, tanners, or woodcutters who cut stones as the need arose. They considered themselves to be craftsmen not artisans, and therefore seldom signed their work. Luckily, information about several New England stonecutting families has survived, though records are too meager to do more than locate them in certain time frames and towns.

According to research done by Reverend Ralph Tucker, Joseph Sikes came from a stonecutting family that was active in Vermont, Connecticut, Massachusetts, and Maine. Through records found in Bristol, Maine, it is believed that Joseph was the son who was active here. In Scarborough, his stones date from the 1760s to 1797. The oval-shaped heads, tiny mouths, semi-circular, eyes and unique hairstyles make his stones easy to recognize. His carvings employ suns, moons, six-pointed stars, grapes, vines, and lots of hearts. The sorrowful characters may appear alone or with as many as four to a stone. There is no signature shape to his stones, which have a variety of silhouettes.

Sikes used poor-quality stone that is rapidly deteriorating, but there are still many legible samples here. His finest stone is of a large to assume that many of the barren areas once held headstones. Western Cemetery's chaotic history is outlined in William Jordan's book, *Burial Records 1811–1980 of the Western Cemetery in Portland Maine.* The cemetery opened in 1829, with interments continuing through the 20th century, although few occurred after 1910. Jordan estimates that there are 6,600 graves, but claims that an exact count is impossible due to poor records and general disorganization. An estimated 1600 stones have survived. Burials occurred for ten years before lots were laid out. In 1840 a plan was made with organized plots, lanes, and avenues, but the only copy was destroyed in the Great Fire of 1866, leaving stewards at a loss as to where graves were. From 1829 to 1858, Western was the only Portland cemetery burying the poor and indigent. The unmarked graves of the "stranger's ground" led to further complications when trying to determine possible burial sites. Many people exhumed remains or removed headstones to Evergreen Cemetery, which was far more prestigious, but there are no accurate records. Avenues were used for unmarked burials as they were assured to be empty. Confusion reigned until 1888, when interments were confined to family lots and tombs.

An example of the confused record keeping occurred when the Longfellow tomb, which can be found by following the road to the right after entering, was opened for repairs and found to be empty. No one knows when it happened or where the bodies went. It contained five Longfellows including Henry Wadsworth Longfellow's parents.

Across from the tombs, towards the center, notice the unusual coffin-shaped tomb with the Celtic cross. Gaelic writing and Celtic designs adorn the base.

There are veterans here from the Revolution, the War of 1812, the Spanish-American War, and the Civil War. Maine state law obligates every municipality to designate and maintain veterans' graves, plus decorate each marker on Memorial Day with an American flag. This may be a nearly impossible task in Western, considering the lack of accurate burial accounts. Though not a veteran, Sarah Crossman Hatch is honored for being the daughter of one. In the area of the Celtic-cross tomb is a brass plaque that reads:

Real Daughter
Sarah Crossman Hatch
National Number 42662 NSDAR
Born April 30, 1816 Died March 9, ??

Wife of David S. Hatch
Revolutionary Ancestor, Her Father, Joseph A. Crossman,
A Mariner Who Fought at the Battle of Bunker Hill
Placed by Elizabeth Wadsworth Chapter
NSDAR. May 27, 1987

Following the outside road past the tombs and to the street side, notice the monument erected to Henry Jackson, "a teacher of Grammar for twenty-five years." Just past his memorial are the gravestones of the Kellogg family. Elijah Kellogg (1813–1901) was a Bowdoin College and Andover Theologian graduate and an ordained minister in Harpswell. He also served as chaplain for Boston's Seaman's Friends Society and in Boston's Mariner Church. Kellogg is best known as the author of *Spartacus to the Gladiators*, and was widely recognized during his time as a writer of popular boy's stories. He also acted as a mentor to "irascible" boys, an idea that is currently being revisited. Bowdoin College has an extensive collection of his personal documents, manuscripts, sermons, and records.

In the barren middle section is a stone that was too tough for even the meanest vandals. It is granite cut in the shape of a slate, with a high tympanum and weird oversized lettering. It is interesting that the stone predates the cemetery. It states:

Jonathan
Drefser
died Oct
ye 12th AD 1800
in the 76 year
of his age

The best aspect of Western Cemetery is the "Old Catholic Ground." It is the area along Vaughan Street near the corner of the Western Promenade. It was designated for Catholic burials, and from 1843 to 1882 approximately nine hundred Irish Catholics were buried here, often several in a single grave. Only fifty-seven headstones have been located.

The Irish buried here had escaped the potato famine, and they arrived hungry and destitute. They are honored by the monument erected in 2000 by the Ancient Order of Hibernians (AOH). *The Western Cemetery Project 1997–2001 Irish-American History,* is a publication that outlines the efforts made by the AOH to document burials, clean stones, and erect the monument. The AOH is a Catholic lay organization that can trace its roots back to 1641, originating as a secret society formed to protect themselves and their religion from the English and the Protestant Reformation.

This stunning polished granite monument honors the Irish immigrants who came to Portland to escape the Potato Famine.

The monument is sandblasted with a famished woman and her two children. It reads:

An Gorta Mor (The Great Hunger)
Sacred to the Memory of the Irish Who Perished
During, or Fled Hunger, Disease, an Artificial Famine and
Oppressive Laws During the Great Hunger in Ireland.
Erected by AOH & Dedicated in 2000
as Part of Their Western Cemetery Project to
Clean Gravestones & Record Carvings
& Trace as Many Burials as Possible.

One of the most beautiful stones in this section is a large slate near the outer road parallel to Western Promenade. It is carved with a cross, I H S (a contracted spelling of Jesus in Greek, which has become a symbol for Jesus.), and other symbols. The inscription reads:

In memory of
Rachel McCauley,
daughter of
John & Jane McCauley,

who dept. this life July 26, 1837,
aged 3 years & 7 mos.
Oh! Lovely babe our fond delight
From us was snatched away
To heaven's bright throne with God to dwell
And praise him night and day.

The Catholic headstones are easily identified as they tend to have crosses, and/or I H S or *Requiescant in Pace*, which means "rest in peace" in Latin. There are also references to the Irish counties of origin: Bellmount, Louth, Meath, Galway, and Limerick. A bit of local tradition survives from this cemetery, which rests on an area that used to be called Brown's Hill. Older Irish folks still refer to death or dying as "Going over to Brown's Hill."

Through the 20th century, Portland neglected Western Cemetery, leaving it to vagrants and vandals. Due to pressure exerted by Jordan and like-minded people, the cemetery was finally mowed and cleaned. Today, Western Cemetery is a safe place to visit and efforts continue to maintain it. Broken headstones remain as evidence of past destruction, and liquor bottles and litter still appear behind stones. A visit to Western Cemetery is a reminder of the ways that we both honor and dishonor our dead.

Gaelic writing and Celtic designs adorn the base of this unusual coffin-shaped tomb.

Also of Interest:

The **Portland Museum of Art** is housed in an award-winning building designed by I. M. Pei & Partners. The inside is just as impressive, with its collection of fine and decorative arts dating from the 18th century to the present. Maine's local art is well represented, with works by Winslow Homer, John Singer Sargent, Rockwell Kent, Marsden Hartley, and Andrew Wyeth. Open Tuesday through Sunday year-round and on Mondays in the summer. Hours are 10:00 to 5:00 and on Fridays 10:00 to 9:00. 7 Congress Square, Portland. Tel: (207) 775-6148. Website: *www.portlandmuseum.org*.

At 270 acres, **Evergreen Cemetery** is one of New England's largest burial grounds. Established in 1852, it was designed in the grand style of Mount Auburn Cemetery in Cambridge, Massachusetts. It is the final home to many of Portland and Maine's most interesting people, as well as a recommended stop for bird watchers. Stevens Avenue, Portland.

Portland
EASTERN CEMETERY

Directions: From Route 1, follow Route 1A to Franklin Arterial. At the intersection of Franklin Arterial and Congress Street, turn right onto Congress if coming from Commercial Street and left if coming from Marginal Way. The cemetery will be on your right after several blocks. The key to the cemetery is kept at the Carlson and Turner Bookstore across the street, open Monday through Saturday.

Portland's Eastern Cemetery is one of Maine's most interesting historical burial grounds. At six acres, it is small enough to be easily navigated, but large enough to offer a wide assortment of stones, epitaphs, carvings, and stories. It is located on Munjoy Hill, an older neighborhood. Views from the cemetery are not beautiful, but they are fascinating. To the rear, on the crest of the hill, is the Portland Observatory, and to the front is Portland's working harbor, dressed with a huge oil rig, a cruise ship, ferries, tugs, pleasure craft, and an assortment of fishing vessels.

Eastern Cemetery is fronted by Portland's busy harbor.

Eastern Cemetery was established in 1668, though burials occurred earlier. Most burials ceased by the mid-1800s with the establishment of Western Cemetery in 1829, Evergreen Cemetery in 1852, and Forest City in 1858. In fact, Eastern lost population to Evergreen Cemetery, which was modeled after Mount Auburn in Cambridge, Massachusetts. Some of the city's more prominent families exhumed bodies or simply removed stones in order to create family plots in the more prestigious Evergreen Cemetery. On one other occasion Eastern lost population, though in a much more gruesome way. During the rebuilding after the Great Fire of 1866, a plan was made to connect Mountfort and Federal streets. In order for that to occur, the city removed the back side of the cemetery—bones, coffins, corpses, earth—and used it as landfill in the Back Cove area. Reports vary about how much was removed, with estimates ranging between twelve and fifty feet. No records survive of how many bodies were removed.

It is believed that there are well over four thousand bodies buried in Eastern, though there is no way to accurately determine the number, as record keeping throughout its history has been shoddy and haphazard. According to William Jordan, author of *Burial Records 1717-1962 of Eastern Cemetery Portland Maine,* records of interment locations were not started until 1772. Jordan believes that vandals have destroyed approximately two-thirds of the stones. Vandalism and neglect have been issues in Eastern since 1816, when the first reference to vandalism appeared. In 1828, an editorial expressing outrage at the cemetery's vandals was printed, and in 1846 the *Tribune & Bulletin* published a plea to the city to adorn the cemetery to make it more appealing. The unknown author writes, "Flowers are afraid to blush and grass grows sparingly—where birds refuse to sing, and even the reptiles are sluggish and mute—where the clouds drop no fatness and the sun scorches to desolation—where the breath of God's displeasure seems to linger, as on the plains of Sodom. Say, ye fathers of our city, shall not a green thing be planted in our graveyard?" The neglect and vandalism that occurred in the late 20th century has been by far the most devastating and horrifying. Vandals destroyed hundreds of stones and broke into the ninety-five underground tombs. Silver hinges and handles were stolen off caskets, bones were strewn about, and Commander Preble's wife's casket was used for firewood. Currently, the locked cemetery is faring better than in previous times, largely due to William Jordan's tireless efforts to keep the historical significance, as well as the neglect, of both Eastern and Western cemeteries in the news.

One of Eastern's unique features is that two sections were set aside as "colored ground" in the early 19th century for African-American burials. One section is at the corner of Federal and

Mountfort streets and the other is at Congress and Mountfort streets. Most of the graves are unmarked. Records indicate name and race, but not the burial site.

In the section at the corner of Congress and Mountfort Streets, which is the left-hand corner after entering, is the new stone for James Bowes. The original stone stated:

James Bowes
Revolutionary War
Pensioner
Very Aged
1800
Colored

Also in this area are Janette and William Ruby, the African-American wife and son of Reuben Ruby, a prominent abolitionist, who made a modest strike during the Gold Rush in 1849.

John Brown Russwurm (1799–1851) was the son of a black Jamaican mother and a white father, John Russwurm, who is buried here, though his stone has been destroyed. When Russwurm left Jamaica, he sent his son to school in Canada. When he married a Maine woman, she insisted that John Brown join them and take his father's name of Russwurm. After the death of her husband, she remarried but continued to care for John. He graduated from Bowdoin College in 1826 and is thought to be the country's third man of African descent to finish college and the first to graduate from Bowdoin, where he gave the commencement speech at his graduation.

In 1795, a Quaker section was established, but keeping with Quaker tradition, they were buried without markers. The section is believed to be along the fence on Mountfort Street, though records do not indicate an exact location or the number of Quaker burials that occurred.

It is known that Eastern, like most cemeteries of the period, had several areas set aside as "strangers' ground," but the locations have been lost. Jordan speculates that many of the poor or unclaimed were buried beneath the paths that divide the graveyard.

There are several interesting memorial dedications. The Elizabeth Wadsworth Chapter of the Daughters of the American Revolution erected a monument dedicated to those who fought in the "War of Independence" in 1909. Another monument at the entrance is a bronze plague inscribed with the following:

> Eastern Cemetery
> Chartered in 1668
> Declared a National Historic Site January 1974
> Here lie the hardy courageous early settlers
> the men and women who formed and defended
> this area, who made history in civil life,
> government, law, the arts, education, religion,
> in the state and in the nation.
> 3848 named graves including
> defenders of the colonial wars,
> 150 soldiers of the Revolution,
> defenders of the War of 1812, The Civil War
> and 206 unnamed graves of early settlers.
> To them this tablet is dedicated
> by the Longfellow Garden Club
> July 1975

A monument of note belongs to Alonzo P. Stinson, found at the corner of Congress and Mountfort streets. It can be recognized by the carved sleeping roll and bronze medallion portrait. It states:

> Alonzo P. Stinson
> Third Sergeant Company H
> Fifth Regiment
> Maine Volunteer Infantry
> Aged 19 Years
> Killed First Battle Bull Run
> July 21st 1861
> Sergeant Stinson was the First
> Volunteer Soldier from
> Portland
> to Give His Life for
> the Preservation of the Union
> in the Civil War
> This Memorial Erected by the
> Survivors of Company H
> Present to the City of Portland
> July 4, 1908

Portland's favorite son is the poet, Henry Wadsworth Longfellow.

His grandfather, General Peleg Wadsworth, who is buried in Eastern, was a captain during the Revolution and second in command of the unsuccessful Penobscot Expedition against the British in Castine in 1779.

Longfellow's uncle, Lieutenant Henry Wadsworth, is also memorialized here. He was an eleven-year naval officer who lost his life in 1804 during the Tripoli War. His ship, the *Intrepid*, was blown up to avoid capture by the Barbary Pirates. His marker has been destroyed, but still standing is the headstone of his officer, Commander Edward Preble. Preble led the fleet against the Barbary Pirates and was skipper of the USS *Constitution* or *Old Ironsides*. Preble is sometimes referred to as the "Father of the American Navy." He died in 1807 at the youthful age of 46.

Near the center of the cemetery is a handsome pink granite monument with metal inlays that belongs to James Alden, also of naval fame. Alden is a direct descendent of John Alden the *Mayflower* Pilgrim. From 1838 to 1842, Alden was lieutenant on an expedition that explored the Antarctic and the Hawaiian, Fuji, and Samoan islands. In 1844, he embarked on a successful voyage around the world on the *Constitution*. Later, in the Civil War battle of Mobile Bay, Alden was in the column leading the fleet to battle. When the ship ahead of him was sunk, and he heard reports of torpedoes being used, he panicked and started to back up his ship, throwing the rest of the fleet into disarray. His action provoked Commander Farragut on the *Hartford* to sail to the head of the column and declare his famous statement, "Damn the torpedoes! Go ahead!" In spite of his mistake and the controversy it inspired after the battle, Alden rose to rear admiral and retired in 1872.

One of the best stories found in Maine's cemeteries is the tale of two young sea captains who fought for opposing countries during the War of 1812 but lie buried side by side. On September 5, 1813, the British brig *Boxer* and the American ship *Enterprise* engaged in a battle near Monhegan Island and forty miles from Portland. An eighteen-pound shot instantly killed the British commander, Captain Blyth. The American, Captain Burrows, was mortally wounded and died eight hours later. Captain Burrows refused to be taken below until the *Boxer* surrendered. His wish was fulfilled when he was presented with Captain Blyth's sword, to which he responded, " I am satisfied. I die contented."

The next morning the *Enterprise* sailed to Union Wharf in

Portland Harbor, with the *Boxer* in submission. The public was allowed on board as part of the victory celebration. Both sea captains were given a full military funeral that was a huge community event drawing people from all walks of life and from the surrounding countryside. Solemn music and the firing of guns by two artillery companies marked the lengthy funeral procession, while all the ships in the harbor flew their colors at half mast. Each casket was draped with the captain's national flag, and six volleys were shot over the graves.

In Henry Wadsworth Longfellow's poem "My Lost Youth," he recalls the event in the following stanza:

> I remember the sea fight far away,
> How it thundered o'er the tide!
> And the dead captains, as they lay
> In their grave, o'er looking the tranquil bay,
> Where they in battle died.

The crew of the *Boxer* immediately erected a memorial for their fallen captain, but it was not until years later that a stranger donated money for a similar memorial for Burrows. A monument was also erected for Lieutenant Waters, who was mortally wounded in the battle. The three boxlike monuments have brick bases with marble-slab tops and are at the top of the rise near Mountfort Street. They appear to have been redone as they are in excellent condition. The British commander's inscription reads:

> In Memory
> of
> Captain Samuel Blyth
> Late Commander
> of
> His Britannic Majesty's Brig Boxer
> He nobly fell
> On the 5th day of September 1813
> In action
> With the U.S. Brig Enterprise.
> In life Honorable!
> In death glorious!
> His country will long deplore one of her bravest Sons
> His friends long lament one of the best of Men
> æt. 29

The surviving officers of his crew offer this
feeble tribute of admiration and respect

Burrows' inscription reads:

Beneath this Stone
moulders
the body
of
Captain William Burroughs
Late Commander
of the
United States Brig Enterprise
who was mortally wounded
On the 5th of Sept. 1813.
in an action which contributed
to increase the fame of
American valor by capturing
His Britannic Majesty's
Brig Boxer
after a severe contest of
forty-five minutes
Aet. 28

A passing stranger has erected this memorial of respect to the
memory of a Patriot, who in the hour of peril obeyed the loud
summons of an injured country, and who gallantly met, fought
and conquered the foeman.

And the midshipman's:

Beneath this stone
by the side of his Gallant Commander
rest the remains of
Lieut. Kevin Waters
A native of Georgetown, District of
Columbia, who received a mortal
wound, Sept. 5, 1813
while a midshipman aboard the
U.S. Brig Enterprise
in an action with His B.M. Brig Boxer
which terminated in the capture
of the latter

He languished in severe pain
which he endured with fortitude
until Sept. 25, 1813
when he died with christain
calmness of resignation
Aged 18
The young men of Portland
erect this stone
as a testimony of their respect
for his valour and virtues.

The oldest stones are found to the far right, behind the brick building. There is a beautiful array of carvings to enjoy, including death heads, winged cherubs, urns, and an interesting "purple" headstone carved with a man's profile.

There are many tales of infants' deaths and people lost at sea, and at times both, as in the following inscription:

An elaborately carved winged cherub adorns this gravestone in Eastern Cemetery.

In Memory of
Mrs. Eliza S. Hayden
wife of Mr. Josiah Hayden
aged 21 years:
Robert Stonehouse,
their son, aged 10 months
They were wrecked on
Richmonds Island July 12, 1807
with Capt. Jacob Adams
of Schr. Charles;
where 13 others perished

The following inscription marks the same shipwreck, as the dates are the same. The woman bears the same name as the child above and their stones are near each other. Is it possible she was his grandmother?

In Memory Of
Mrs. Mary Stonehouse
She was drowned from the
Portland Packet July 12

1807: aged 62 years
From the cold bosom of the wave,
Where others found a watr'y grave,
This lifeless corpse was borne! & here,
The friends of virtue drop the tear
That mourne the much lamented dead,
But, ah! what bitter tears are shed
For fathers, mothers, babes who sleep
In the dark mansions of the deep!

There are an incredible number of tragedies found etched into gravestones, but occasionally an epitaph resonates with simple joy. A small marble stone from 1853 states merely:

Thankful

Eastern Cemetery is forlorn and quite homely. The words of our unknown author are as true today as in 1846, " ... grass grows sparingly—where birds refuse to sing ..." Yet, it is also a thoroughly captivating burial ground filled with historic stories of life, death, and heroics. Hopefully the City of Portland finally understands its obligation to preserve and protect this invaluable landmark.

Though Eastern Cemetery is poorly maintained, its history is captivating.

Also of Interest:

General Peleg Wadsworth, the grandfather of Henry Wadsworth Longfellow, built the **Wadsworth Longfellow House** in 1785. The Federal-style home is where the poet spent much of his childhood and is now a memorial that allows visitors to glimpse his life through guided tours. Open June through October. Monday through Saturday, from 10:00 to 4:00. Sunday, from 12:00 to 4:00. Next door is the **Center for Maine History**, with changing exhibits highlighting Maine's history. Open year-round, Monday through Saturday, from

10:00 to 5:00. Sundays in the summer, from 12:00 to 5:00. Behind the house and museum is the **Maine Historical Society Library**. The research library is an excellent source for those pursuing genealogy or any type of research related to Maine. It houses 125,000 books, 2 million manuscripts, and approximately 8,000 artifacts. Open year-round. Tuesday through Saturday, from 10:00 to 4:00. All three are found at 489 Congress Street, Portland. Tel: (207) 774-1822. *www.mainehistory.org* or *www.mainememory.net.*

Yarmouth
Old Ledge Cemetery

***Directions: From Route 1 in Yarmouth, turn onto Route 88
south. At the 'V' of Route 88 and Gilman Road, the cemetery
will be on the left.***

Yarmouth is a bustling coastal town that once was a major shipbuilding center and home to an assortment of factories, mills, and
canneries. The combination of the Royal River and the Atlantic Ocean
created steady employment and prosperity. The rich heritage of
Yarmouth's early days is reflected in a number of engaging burial
grounds. The setting and historic graves make Old Ledge Cemetery
stand out from the others.

Pastoral Old Ledge
Cemetery is framed by rolling
fields and a view of the bay.
Graves date from 1736 to
approximately 1915, with the
majority of markers belonging to
the 19th century. You will find the
work of a well-known stonecutter, interesting death heads, and
many marble stones and granite
monuments here.

*The oldest gravestone at Old Ledge Cemetery
is dated 1736.*

Near the cemetery center
are nine stones carved by Noah
Pratt, Jr., who along with his family has a certain degree of fame in
stonecutting history. Noah Pratt
Jr. settled in Freeport between
1781 and 1791. There are approximately forty stones in Maine that
can be attributed to him. Like
Joseph Sikes, Pratt used a poor quality of stone and time is rapidly taking its toll on these charming markers.

Time is rapidly taking its toll on Noah Pratt Jr.'s stones, visible in the foreground.

Pratt's stones are easily identified, even when the carving is indistinct, by their high tympanum (center arch) and decorated finials (side treatments). Reverend Ralph Tucker compiled characteristics typical of Pratt's work. Often, a halo of leaves surrounds the portrait and sometimes there are six pointed stars on the tops of the tympanum and finials. His male portraits depict a head with identifiable hair on a narrow neck, with the man either facing the viewer or in profile. The females face the viewer and wear hoods covering their hair. There are several portraits in the Old Ledge Cemetery, but because they are somewhat worn, the best viewing is in bright afternoon sunlight or in the morning with a mirror. (See Freeport's Mast Landing Cemetery for more photographs of Pratt's carvings.)

I found several renditions of the 18th-century classic epitaph that expresses so well the Congregationalist belief that death must be diligently prepared for.

From 1793:

> Come my dear friends, prepare to die
> Prepare to dwell with God on high
> Get union with the Lord divine

59

Then leave your bodies here with mine
From 1788:
My loving friends as you pass by
On my cold grave pray cast an eye
Your sun like mine may set at noon
Your soul be called for very soon
In this dark place you'll quickly be
Prepare for death and follow me

From 1799:

To time and toil I've bid adieu
I lie in dust tho' once like you,
And you like me shall quickly have
Your lodging in the silent grave
Think of your end, rest not secure
But make your salvation sure

The 18th-century epitaphs were meant as warnings to the living and not to commemorate the deceased. In many places, the 19th century brought a move away from epitaphs that warned of impending death toward more optimistic epitaphs about a glorious afterlife. At times, this less fearful attitude towards death was replaced with pessimism towards life, as in the following epitaph from 1803.

Lean not on earth; 'Twill pierce thee to The heart
A broken staff at best and oft a spear
On its sharp point peace bleeds and hope expires

The same pessimism is evident in the following epitaph from 1818 that mourns the death of a 20-month-old child.

So fades the lovely blooming flower
Frail, smiling solace of our home
So soon our transient comforts fly
And pleasure only blooms to die.

Notice that in places large granite blocks serve as a single replacement for several older stones and are carved with names and dates spanning generations. Families have exercised their rights to remove original stones. Hopefully this will not be a trend, as polished black granite is much less appealing than the soft white marble of the graveyard's era.

There is a rich span of history to enjoy in this peaceful setting. The number of epitaphs and variety of markers create compelling reasons for exploring the grounds.

Also of Interest:

The **Museum of Yarmouth History**, established by the Yarmouth Historical Society, is on the third floor of the impressive Merrill Memorial Library. It is a treasure trove of documents, artifacts, manuscripts, and photographs, and features changing exhibitions of local history and art. They are currently updating all cemetery records and dedicated volunteers are copying the inscriptions from the markers in Yarmouth's historic cemeteries. Open July and August, Monday through Friday from 1:00 to 5:00. September to June, Tuesday through Friday from 1:00 to 5:00 and Saturdays from 10:00 to 5:00. 215 Main Street, Yarmouth. Tel: (207) 846-6259.

Yarmouth

PIONEERS' BURIAL GROUND OR THE INDIAN FIGHTERS' BURIAL GROUND

Directions: Follow directions to Old Ledge Cemetery. The graveyard is 100 yards from Old Ledge on Gilman Road.

The Pioneers' Burial Ground is a tiny cemetery of two-dozen slate stones, though it is obvious that there are unmarked graves here as well. The slate tablets are carved with death heads and range in date from 1731 to 1774, with the majority dating from the 1730s through the 1750s.

Small Pioneers' Burial Ground has only two-dozen gravestones.

The grave of Deacon Mitchell is one of only three documented burials for a person who lived beyond the age of sixty.

Being very old, the stones are best viewed in bright afternoon sunlight or with a mirror in the morning. In the center is a monument that reads:

> The Pioneers
> Burial Ground
> Here rest those who in
> the third and permanent
> settlement of the town
> defended it against the
> savage enemies, some at
> the sacrifice of their lives

Records at the Museum of Yarmouth History indicate that the majority of those buried here died in their twenties, forties, or as children. There are only three known burials of people over the age of sixty. In this small cemetery I can only wonder if those buried here had anticipated the degree of bravery that would be required of them as pioneers in New England.

Yarmouth
BAPTIST CEMETERY

Directions: From Route 1 in Yarmouth, turn onto Route 115 west, West Main Street. Turn right onto Hill Street. The cemetery is on the right, next to the Old Baptist Meetinghouse.

Baptist Cemetery is one of the few where the stones face east, so morning is the best time for viewing and photographing.

The Old Baptist Meetinghouse and the adjoining cemetery were established in 1796. The cemetery is mid-sized and features predominately 19th century stones, with 20th century stones towards the back. An initial count by volunteers for the Yarmouth Historical Society has recorded the burials of eighty-three veterans: six from the American Revolution, eleven from the War of 1812, forty-four from the Civil War, and the remaining from 20th-century wars. The marble and slate stones exhibit all the stone-cutting fashions of the 1800s. Though the stones vary in their legibility, there is plenty of reading to occupy visitors. Be sure to notice the humble hand-carved stone on the left as you enter the cemetery.

All of the slate tablets are of the willow and urn design, but were probably cut by a variety of carvers as they exhibit different renditions of the classic style. Following the Revolutionary War, the willow and urn motif, portrayed singularly or together, came to dominate gravestone carvings. During this period, the excavation of Pompeii and Herculaneum in the mid-1700s triggered widespread interest in ancient Greece and Rome and strongly influenced European and American cultures. The willow and urn were reflections of the neoclassic art and ideas that were pervasive from approximately 1750 to 1850. Also, secularism became more pervasive as the Unitarian and

Universalist churches and the influences of the Enlightenment spread. The winged cherub and its flight to heaven gradually disappeared and was replaced by the willow and urn, symbolizing earthly grief over mortal remains.

There are tales of dramatic deaths found on many of the headstones. Miranda J. Winslow's story is tragic. Her and her children's stones are towards the back, on the left. Note that her first child drowned several months before Miranda and her two toddlers suffered the same fate. Another child's grave is in the grouping, but leaves no clue as to the cause of death. Miranda's epitaph reads:

> The voice oft has answered mine
> Earth cannot now reclaim
> Nor ever will thy own sweet smile
> Part those sealed lips again.

There are others who have left tales of dramatic deaths. In 1836, a 24-year-old "died of Yellow Fever in New Orleans." A 26-year-old, a member of the famed 20th Regiment Maine Volunteers, Company K, died in 1864 from wounds "at the Battle of the Wilderness, Va." In 1847, a 35-year-old man lost his life by "an explosion of the Steamboat *Edna* opposite the town of Columbia, upon the Ouchilia." Death and grief were then as they are now, bound in disease, war, and random accident.

The Brooks family monument is an outstanding white bronze. Each of the four sides has a different yet equally appealing design. It can be found towards the left front.

The North Yarmouth and Freeport Old Baptist Meetinghouse is Yarmouth's historic pride and joy. It was built on a hill as protection against attack, and typical to the period, it was used as both a meetinghouse and a church. It has been lovingly maintained for its historical significance since 1949. Be sure to

The white bronze, or zinc, monument for the Brooks family is adorned on all four sides.

notice the outstanding weathervane that is thought to be the original. Though meetinghouses are uniformly white now, originally they were brown, red, or yellow. It was the rusticators of the late 1800s who changed the landscape of color with their romanticized visions of colonial times. During the Colonial Revival, many meetinghouses were architecturally "updated" and painted white. This meetinghouse was last remodeled and enlarged in 1837, somehow escaping the attention of the Revivalists.

The Baptist Cemetery is one of the few cemeteries where the stones face east, so morning is the best time for visibility and photographs. Enjoy the many inscriptions, along with the fine examples of urn and willow slates and Victorian marbles.

Freeport
WOODLAWN CEMETERY

Directions: From Route 1 in Freeport Village, turn onto West Street. The cemetery is up one block on the right.

Freeport is a treasure on the coast of southern Maine. Many know it only as the home of L. L. Bean and as a retail outlet mecca. But if you wander off Route 1, you'll find beautiful parks, plenty of quintessential Maine coastline, and lots of history.

Woodlawn Cemetery rates as one of the more unusual burying grounds because of its two distinct personalities. The center is groomed, refined, and picturesque, while the outskirts are rough and tumble. Along the center driveway the grounds are well maintained with interesting plantings and a nice mixture of 19th- and 20th-century markers. Appealing contemporary stones rest side by side with older marbles. But move to the edges and you'll find thick beds of moss, tilt-

ing and sinking stones, foxholes, an abandoned shed, and a paupers' patch. Woodlawn has an intangible quality that brings together disparate elements. Stones that are askew look like part of the landscape instead of like neglect. The forest borders one side, while a homely chain-link fence closes in the other. There is an amazing mixed bag here: 19th-century monuments, traditional marble slabs that are softening and toppling, lichen-covered stones blackened with age, contemporary shiny granite blocks, salmon granite, and at least one very large Maine boulder.

Move through the groomed center to the springy fairyland in

Some of the tumbled stones at Woodlawn have actually become part of the landscape.

the back and out again to the forlorn pauper's patch along the chain-link fence. Here a jumble of small stones lines the fence in unkempt disarray. Out of the fourteen legible stones, eight are for children, three are for young adults and three are for adults. When the cemetery was organized, lot 15 was set aside for paupers or those who were not claimed by family. There were seventeen recorded burials in lot 15.

The north section of the graveyard was originally the family burial ground for Simeon Coffin. In 1857, his land, along with the holdings of several others, was acquired to create the cemetery. The original town burial ground was on Bow Street, but it was decided that it was better suited as a park, so in 1873, 125 bodies were moved to Woodlawn Cemetery. The oldest re-interred grave belonged to Samuel Litchfield, who was a Revolutionary War veteran who died in 1797. It is suspected that bodies were disinterred carelessly or not removed at all if there was no marker. Major Thomas Means was a Revolutionary War veteran and a man held in high esteem, yet his and one of his wives' bodies are in an unknown location.

A taste of contemporary Maine culture can be witnessed at the Coffin family plot. The large granite block depicts a hunting scene and the epitaph reads:

> Wisdom is knowing what to do
> Skill is knowing
> How to do it and
> Virtue is doing it well.

On his stone is carved a rifle, and on hers, a rose.

Woodlawn Cemetery has a unique presence that sets it apart from others. A quick drive thru will not do justice to all that is here to explore.

Also of Interest:

Freeport is blessed with the active **Freeport Historical Society,** which has an avid interest in preserving its twenty-two cemeteries. They will even supply you with a map to help you find them. They hold the research papers of Reverend Ralph Tucker, who carefully documented information about stonecutters and grave carvings, plus they have supplementary information on the cemeteries and the families you'll find in them. From July to December they feature exhibits on local history, and from January to May they have changing exhibits of local artists. Tuesday through Friday from 10:00 to 2:00 or by appointment. 45 Main Street, Freeport. Tel: 207-865-3170. *www.frphistory@aol.com.*

Woodlawn Cemetery has a nice mixture of 19th- and 20th-century stones.

Freeport
MAST LANDING CEMETERY

***Directions: I-95 to I-295, to Exit 20, Freeport. Follow Route 1
north. Turn right onto Upper Mast Landing Road. The cemetery is approximately .5 mile on the left.***

Freeport's most distin-
guished graveyard is the
Mast Landing Cemetery.
The cemetery is tucked
into a historic area that
is named in reference to
the huge white pines
that were cut nearby
and rafted down the
Harraseeket River to
supply England with ship
masts during the 1700s.
This small cemetery of

Mast Landing is Freeport's most historic cemetery.

approximately 120 burials has stones carved by Noah Pratt, Jr. and
graves that date from 1784 to 1903. There are three Revolutionary
War veterans and five from the War of 1812.

*The gravestone of Captain Abner
Dennison was carved by Noah
Pratt, Jr.*

The oldest stone in the Mast Landing
Cemetery is Mary Dennison's, who died in
1784. The stone is at the top of the hill, in
a line of four stones, three of which are
believed to be carved by Noah Pratt Jr. As
in Yarmouth, the Pratt headstones are
badly eroded, but due to their high tympanum they are easy to identify. (See Ledges
Cemetery in Yarmouth for information on
Noah Pratt Jr.) Mary Dennison, who died
at 26 years of age, is between her in-laws.
She and her father-in-law have Pratt
stones, while her mother-in-law was
buried much later and has a slate stone.

70

Captain Abner Dennison's classic epitaph reads:

Remember this you passerby
As you are now so wonce (sic) was I
As I am so Must you be
Prepare for death, O Follow me

The Reverend Ralph Tucker found that all of Pratt Jr.'s footstones followed the same pattern. They are carved only with the name, date of death, straight borders outlining the stone, and a half circle in the tympanum. From this information it can be concluded that Captain Abner

The characteristic high tympanum of a stone carved by Noah Pratt, Jr.

Dennison's footstone is at the end of the row next to his wife's grave, which makes me wonder how many of the stones are in their original positions. When old graveyards have stones that neatly line up, it can be suspected that the stones were moved at some point in time to make mowing easier. Also note that Mary's footstone is in front of her grave instead of to the back. Graveyards sometimes have more footstones than headstones, and in at least one of these cases there is a known reason. The footstone for Zilpha Curtis, also carved by Pratt Jr. is still at Mast Landing, but the headstone is at the Freeport Historical Society and can be viewed if you ask. It is a wonderful example of Pratt's work, with the inscription enclosed in a heart. The stone made its way to its new home after a particularly nasty ice storm knocked it over and damaged the tympanum.

There are several large Sylvester stones that are impressive due to the quality of the slate, the size, and the willow motif. The fortunate Mr. Samuel Sylvester enjoyed longevity as well as prosperity: he died at 89 in 1854. His stone is a good reproduction, though his wife's is original. Henchman and Esther Sylvester have attractive slates where the willow-tree trunks flow down the sides. Henchman died in 1829 at 71 years of age. His epitaph is as follows:

Oh, he is gone!
His course is finished now, his race is over,
The place which knew him, knows him now no more,
The tree is fall'n confined in narrow bounds,
And there to lie till the last trumpet sounds

Mast Landing Cemetery allows us to time travel. Historic gravestones line a gentle slope surrounded by an authentic New England stone wall. On a quiet street, 19th-century homes hug the perimeters. The Mast Landing Cemetery is a treasure for Freeport and for the rest of us.

Freeport
FREE WILL BAPTIST
OR WARD CEMETERY

Directions: From Route 1, follow the signs for routes 136 and 125. Turn onto Route 136, Durham Road. Pass by the Burr Cemetery on the right, and take the next right onto Griffin Road. The cemetery is on the right, shortly after passing Ledgewood Road.

With it's rough ground and epitaphs hopeful of a better place after death, Ward Cemetery is a melencholy place.

The Free Will Baptist or Ward Cemetery occupies a distressed piece of earth. The land buckles and heaves as if the caskets were fighting their way to the surface. Grass and moss grow in sparse patches, competing with ants for the sandy soil. It's a shady spot guarded by oaks and maples, though beware of the roots that sporadically break the ground's surface.

When I arrived, two workmen were clearing rocks and repairing gravestones that had broken with age. They were laying them horizontally on the ground and removing the bases. On that day, even though attention was being paid, the small cemetery still looked neglected, markers twisting and tilting in random directions. On a subsequent visit, the difference was impressive; all the stones had been straightened, repaired, or laid horizontally on the ground. Acid rain is known to damage gravestones, and laying them horizontally increases their exposure, not just to the rain, but to all the elements, including the maintenance-workers' tools.

The earliest burial occurred in 1811 and the latest in 1941, but most stones range from the mid-19th century to the early 20th century. The markers are marble, with the exception of an interesting zinc monument. Zinc monuments were produced from 1880 to 1920 and were initiated by the foundry industry's desire to expand into the memorial business. They are also referred to as white bronze because they were intended to mimic bronze statues that were regularly used for memorials. The hollow zinc monuments were much less expensive than bronze or stone and easier to ship.

The Free Will Baptist Cemetery has abundant religiously inspired epitaphs that are easy to read. A common theme is the difficulty of life on earth and the desire to be transported to heavenly rewards of promised tranquility. The following example is gentler than most:

The zinc marker for Joseph and Leah Ward is the single exception to the marble stones of the Free Will Baptist Cemetery.

Moses Grant
Died
Dec. 8 1887
Æ 71 yrs.
Go to thy rest in peace,
And soft be thy repose:
Thy toils are o'er thy troubles cease.
From earthly care is thou release
Thine eyelids gently close.

No doubt life was difficult for John and Mary Ward, who lost three children within a month. The daughters' epitaph was popular in the 19th century. It reads:

These lovely buds so young and fair
Called hence by early doom
Just came to share how sweet a flower

In paradise might bloom.

The epitaph on their son's gravestone reads:

Farewell my dear boy thy spirit is free
To dwell with the pure, thy sisters to see
We will not repine, though absent from sight
Since thou art there with angels of light

The Ward cemetery is a melancholy place with its tumultuous ground and epitaphs ever hopeful of a better day. It's not a must-see graveyard, but it is a sacred spot worthy of a visit.

Freeport

POTE CEMETERY

Directions: I-95 to I-295 to Exit 20, Freeport. Follow Route 1 south, and turn left onto Bow Street. Bear right onto Flying Point Road. Turn left onto Wolf's Neck Road. After passing Mayfield Road, the Wolf's Neck Lodge will be on the left. Proceed to the old farmhouse that is less than a mile from the lodge. This is the original Greenfield Pote House. Directly across the street is a narrow road marked "private." (I checked with the town and it is a public road.) Drive up the road to the clearing on the right. If the area is mowed, drive in, if not, walk in.

The Pote Cemetery is named for the gentleman who was the first owner of the oldest standing house in the Wolf's Neck area of Freeport. Captain Greenfield Pote built his home in Falmouth around 1760. Five years later he loaded it onto a flatboat and moved it to its present location in Freeport. What provoked the change of address? Pote, a successful Yankee skipper, took advantage of a favorable sea breeze to arrive home on the Sabbath, only to be greeted by an official complaint and fine for working on the sacrosanct day. Considerably outraged, he moved his home to Freeport.

The family progenitor is the first known burial in the cemetery bearing his name, though his wife is buried in Falmouth. Graves range in date from 1797 to 1921, with one modern exception. Amidst predominately 19th-century stones is an impressive 1995 granite block marking the passage of Virginia Weiner at age 50. She left behind a husband and two children who have created a loving memorial. A small terraced garden encircles a granite bench that faces her gravestone. A rock engraved "Mom's Garden" is tucked amongst lilies, yarrow, lavender, chive, black-eyed Susan, and coreopsis. Treasures of seashells, feathers, and unusual rocks decorate her stone like an ancient altar. There is a meditative quality to the garden that lends itself to mourning, but also to the comfort that comes from cherishing memories of a special woman.

It is common to find stones, pebbles, and shells on Jewish markers. "F.A.Q.—A Question Wrapped in a Conundrum: Why Do Jews put Pebbles on Gravestones?" by Roberta Halporn appeared in one of the Association for Gravestone Studies' quarterly bulletins. Halporn discussed and dismissed two common explanations. The first is that the pebble is left so that the next person to visit the grave is comforted by knowing there have been other visitors. The second is that when Jews were nomadic desert dwellers they buried their dead under

Visitors have placed stones and shells on this Jewish marker at Pote Cemetery.

large stones and then stones were added by subsequent passers-by as blessings. The explanation proposed by Halporn is that the pebble represents a wish for the interred soul to be in the House of God. The pebble derives from the custom of ancient Israelites who raised stones or pillars to represent the House of God.

The rest of the burial ground includes simple stones and stubs from broken, aged stones. The epitaphs are few and mostly illegible. This is not a place to study fascinating gravestones, but to enjoy the unique blend of history and modern memorial. The lovely memorial and the historic Pote graves among the pines are very charming. The pines are tranquil and the bench is comforting.

New Gloucester

PINELAND CEMETERY—MALAGA ISLAND

Directions: From Route 1 in Yarmouth, turn onto Route 115 west. Bear right onto Route 231. After passing Pineland Center, turn left onto a gravel road just before the Webber Cemetery. Follow the road to the back.

Including Pineland Cemetery on this tour is an unusual choice for two reasons: it is a detour from the coast, and it is the cemetery for the Maine School for the Feeble Minded, later renamed the Pownal State School, and later still the Pineland Hospital and Training Ground. Here you will find the graves of those whose bodies were unclaimed by family and who had the misfortune of spending their lives in an institution that was well-intentioned, but modeled on misconceptions about the mentally ill, the poor, the illiterate, and the neglected. Here you will also find the graves of seventeen people who were exhumed from their original burial ground on Malaga Island, thus the justification for including an inland cemetery on a coastal tour. Plus, it is just too compelling a piece of Maine's history to ignore.

Malaga Island was inhabited from the 1860s to 1912 by a community who eked a living out of the sea and worked seasonal mainland jobs when possible. Many of Maine's islands were populated by squatters who established colonies based on fishing, and often they struggled with poverty and harsh circumstances. Times were particularly difficult at the end of the 19th century, when the entire coast of Maine was experiencing economic decline as the shipbuilding that had sustained it began to decline. It was also a hard time for fishermen due to depleted fish stocks and changing American dietary habits.

By the 1890s, pauper rolls had lengthened throughout the state as people requested assistance. Malaga was no different; poverty was part of daily existence. Some Malaga residents turned to Phippsburg for assistance and though initially they were accommodated, Phippsburg came to resent the Malagaites. This wrath ran so deep that in 1900, when Malaga's population reached forty, Phippsburg cut off aid and attempted to prove in court that Malaga actually belonged to Harpswell. When that failed, they turned to the state, and in 1905, in

78

Brunswick

PINE GROVE CEMETERY

Directions: From Route 1, turn onto Maine Street, following the signs for Bowdoin College. Bear left onto Route 24, Bath Road. Pine Grove is the first cemetery on Route 24 after the intersection of Route 123.

A fortuitous conversation with Barbara Desmarais resulted in a tour that brought Pine Grove Cemetery to my attention. Desmarais was a member of the Brunswick Open Space Task Force, which disbanded in 2002 after completing its goals. Brunswick had the wisdom to recognize that cemeteries serve as important open spaces in urban areas and included them in the town's long-range plans. When no one else stepped forward, Demarais volunteered to locate the town's thirty-five cemeteries and compile information about them in a single document that is available at the town hall, library, historical society, and on-line. With amazing efficiency and the help of community volunteers, she completed a record for each cemetery that provides gravestone inscriptions, history, location, and a physical description. Photographs and biographical information are included whenever possible.

In an area that is otherwise congested, walkers frequently take advantage of the open space provided by Pine Grove Cemetery. Though it does not look particularly appealing from the street, once inside it reveals its charms through beautiful monuments that are some of the most elaborate found along the coast. Graves date

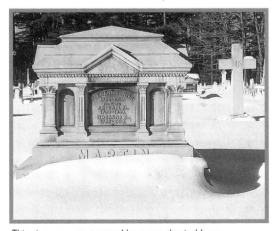

This zinc monument resembles a neo-classical home.

This stunning monument has decidedly Gothic feathures.

from approximately 1801 to 1979, with markers reflecting typical period styles. There is a zinc monument molded into a neoclassical home and a stunning Gothic Revival monument. Many of Brunswick's notable people chose to be buried here. Pine Grove's most frequently visited grave belongs to Joshua Lawrence Chamberlain. The plain granite marker is a short distance from the main entrance, along the right edge. The Pejepscot Historical Society periodically collects pennies that are left on his grave. No doubt the pennies are small tokens left behind to show appreciation for the man who is one of Maine's most revered heroes. He is frequently credited with turning the tide of the Battle of Gettysburg by holding the Union position at Little Round Top, thereby securing the 20th Maine Volunteer Infantry Regiment a place of distinction in history. He rose from lieutenant colonel to major general in four years, during which time he was engaged in twenty-four battles, was wounded six times, and even had his horse shot out from under him six times. At the war's end, General Grant chose Chamberlain to receive the first flag of surrender at Appomattox Courthouse. Known to be a gentleman, Chamberlain ordered his men to salute the defeated Confederates as they marched by.

Chamberlain's success continued in his civilian life. He returned to his pre-war career of teaching rhetoric at his alma mater, Bowdoin

College. Soon he was drawn to Republican politics and served four terms as governor. After politics he returned to Bowdoin as the college president. Due to ill health brought on by his war injuries, he retired in 1883. Business ventures and writing his account of the war kept him active until his death in 1914 at age 85.

Chamberlain's story lives on in John Pullen's book, *Joshua Chamberlain: A Hero's Life and Legacy*. He also plays prominently in the Pulitzer Prize–winning novel, *The Killer Angels*, by Michael Shaara. *Gettysburg*, the 1993 film based on *The Killer Angels*, features both him and his brother Thomas. Thomas Chamberlain is buried in Castine Cemetery.

Next to Chamberlain is the headstone of his wife, Frances Caroline Chamberlain. Her stone is carved with a relief of a laurel wreath and the word "Unveiled," which is especially significant because she was blind at the time of her death.

It will surprise many to learn that Maine had a sizable population of African Americans in the 19th century. H.H. Price and Gerry E. Talbot are currently writing a book on the history of African Americans in Maine. The fascinating information they have collected is changing the perception of Maine's African-American history. As part of their research, they compiled federal census information from 1820 to 1870 and listed each town known to have African American citizens. Brunswick's census indicates a population of at least fifteen, but the cemetery research by Desmarais reveals that the figure is woefully low.

African-American burials are found throughout Brunswick cemeteries, but Phebe Jacobs is particularly interesting because a surviving American Tract Publication titled, "Narrative of Phebe Jacobs," by Mrs. T.C. Opham, provides an insightful look at Jacobs' life and character. Though it is undated, it was probably written shortly after her death in 1850. Her early history was described as follows: "At an early age she was given to Mrs. Wheelock, wife of President Wheelock of Dartmouth college (sic), to be an attendent to her daughter, Maria Malleville, who was afterwards the wife of President Allen's of Bowdoin college (sic), Brunswick, Maine. She came to Brunswick with President Allen's family, in 1820, and remained with them until the death of Mrs. Allen, from which time she chose to live alone." After the death of Maria Allen, Jacobs supported herself by taking in laundry for Bowdoin students.

The narrative is mostly a declaration of Jacob's devout

Christianity. She chose to live alone so that she would be closer to God, prayed three times a day, was a dependable participant in church services, and made monthly fifty-cent contributions to missions. She is described as a woman whose deep faith filled her with joy, compassion, and humility. Jacobs wanted to be buried near to Maria, whom she loved, and her wishes were fulfilled. They are buried next to each other in the Allen family lot. The headstone is in the first lot on the right after entering through the main gate. It reads:

Phebe Ann Jacobs
born a slave
(Illegible)
died Feb. 27, 1870 æt 64

Pine Grove Cemetery is nicely landscaped and well maintained. It reflects the nobility of many of its residents, from several former slaves to two governors. You will also find state and national representatives, college professors, successful entrepreneurs, sea captains, ship builders, town leaders, and many war veterans.

The Heuston Cemetery is an African American cemetery in Brunswick.

Also of Interest:
The **Heuston Cemetery** is a rare find; an African-American cemetery containing approximately thirty graves and seven surviving headstones dating from 1829 to 1926. Michael Mulligan, who is the grandson of the property owners, restored the cemetery in 2002 as his Eagle Scout project. He cleared saplings and brush, reset and cleaned stones, and installed a post and chain fence. These efforts, along with an identifying sign at the entrance, created a charming woodland burial ground.

At one point the Word of God Chapel, which has been moved to Old Bath Road, was nearby. In the late 1880s it had a mixed-race congregation with members from the African-American-owned farms in the area.

The family founder, Francis Heuston, was a successful farmer and owned the land that the burial ground is on. There are two obituaries written about Francis, with the second one correcting the errors in the first, and both leading to some confusion about his life. It is uncertain if he was ever a slave or if he was 94 or 95 at the time of his death. It is known that he worked for many years as a sailor, was a Revolutionary War veteran, had eleven children by two wives, was of impressive size and strength, and was well respected for his integrity. His headstone is lodged in a tree trunk. Buried close to him is his first wife, Mehitable, and his daughter Pamela, who is the first marked burial in 1829. Unfortunately, the Heuston Cemetery is on private property. More information can be found at *www.rootsweb.com/~mebrucem/cem16.html*.

The tree-lodged headstone of Francis Heuston.

The **Pejepscot Museum** serves as the historical society for Brunswick, Harpswell, and Topsham. The museum features changing exhibits of local significance and is also an excellent source for those pursuing genealogy. It houses 50,000 artifacts, more than 20,000 photographs, and an impressive collection of historical records, manuscripts, and documents. A copy of the cemetery records is held here or can be accessed on-line at *www.rootsweb.com/~mebrucem/*. For questions about Brunswick's cemeteries email *brunswick_cemeteries@hotmail.com*. Open year-round. Tuesday through Saturday from 9:00 to 5:00 and Thursday until 8:00. 159 Park Row, Brunswick. Telephone (207) 729-6606. *www.curtislibrary.com/pejepscot.htm*.

Admirers of Joshua Chamberlain will not want to miss the **Joshua L. Chamberlain Museum**. His house was built as a Cape Cod in 1820, but when he bought it in 1871, he elevated it eleven feet and built a new first floor, thereby creating a unique structure. The partially restored home has seven completed rooms with exhibits on Chamberlain's life. Open June 1 through Columbus Day. Tuesday through Saturday from 10:00 to 4:00, with no tickets sold after 3:15. 226 Maine Street, Brunswick.

Harpswell Center
OLD COMMON CEMETERY

Directions: From Route 1 in Brunswick, turn onto Maine Street, following the signs for Bowdoin College. Bear left onto Route 24, Bath Road. Turn right onto Route 123 and follow for approximately 8.3 miles. The cemetery will be on the right, across from the Congregational Church.

A visit to the Old Common Cemetery is a joy due to the $8,000 Harpswell spent in 2001 restoring the gravestones. Cleaning and straightening the stones, trimming the grass, and keeping the woods at bay adds reverence to this cemetery. It is a heartfelt way to honor the dead, as well as the community's history and ancestors. It is also an incredible pleasure to read stones and view carvings without straining to decipher words and images grown thick with lichen.

The burial ground, edged with a thick stone wall, is the perfect backdrop for Harpswell's Old Meetinghouse, built from 1757 to 1759. Approximately six hundred graves date from the mid-1700s to 1900, with more than thirty 18th-century stones. There are an abundance of epitaphs, many of which are poetic and/or inspired by a "glorious resurrection." The epitaphs are often long, so the recent cleaning appreciably eases the task of reading them.

In this image, Harpswell's Old Meetinghouse serves as the perfect backdrop for the Old Common Cemetery.

Harpswell was home to sea captains who sailed over much of the world, and at least six of those captains are buried here. In fact, the Harpswell Historical Society houses a piece of the Rock of Gibraltar brought back by Captain Stephen Johnson. Contact with other cultures and regions often shows itself in graveyards through the materials used for stones, the variety of images, and the degree of sophistication of the cutting. The Old Common Cemetery scores high on all counts. The cemetery has marble, slate, and white-bronze headstones and monuments. Red sandstone, which is common in central Connecticut but not used along the coast of Maine, is found here. There

The winged cherub on this stone wears an elaborate headdress.

are fine examples of winged death heads, winged souls, and a winged death head with crossbones, as well as Victorian relief carvings. One headstone carved in 1786 utilizes the popular cherub icon, but its plumed headdress gives it a decidedly Incan look. Another well-carved stone depicts a setting (or rising) sun with eyes peaking over the horizon. Since Harpswell was once part of North Yarmouth, as Freeport was, it makes sense that there are two Noah Pratt, Jr. stones, though they are in very poor condition. (See Ledges Cemetery in Yarmouth for more about Noah Pratt Jr.)

One of the oldest headstones belongs to Reverend Elisha Eaton, who was employed by Harpswell in 1753. He and his son took two years to build the meetinghouse, where he reigned until his death in 1764. His large slate stone is well carved with a winged cherub and can be found behind the meetinghouse. Close by is his wife Katherine's slate headstone, which reads:

To the memory of
Mrs. Katherine Eaton
the virtuous Relic of the Rev. Mr.
Elisha Eaton, who departed
this Life April 12, 1767, æ 61,

Here Passenger, confined reduced to Dust
Lies what was once religious, wise and just
Fixt (sic) in deep slumbers here the Dust is giv'n
Til the last trumpet shakes the Frame of Heav'n
Then fresh to life the waking Saint shal
l rise
And in new Triumphs glitter up the Skies.
Like her be virtuous, you like her shall shine
In Bliss above, immortal & divine

One of the oldest stones in Harpswell belongs to Reverend Elisha Eaton, who died in 1764.

The Eaton's son Samuel graduated from Harvard, where he studied law, medicine, and ministry. After his father's death he became Harpswell's pastor, but he was also a practicing lawyer and doctor. Samuel's wig and baptismal bowl are stored in the meetinghouse. His inscription reads:

Rev. Samuel Eaton
The 2d Minister of Harpswell
born Apl 3, 1737
graduated at Harvard College 1763:
ordained Oct 21, 1764
& died Nov 5, 1822
in the 86th year of his age
& 59th of his ministry.
Blessed are the dead which die in the Lord

Benjamin Dunning was a Revolutionary War veteran whose virtue epitaph is coupled with a poetic and religious expression of grief typical to the era and particularly to this cemetery. His epitaph contains a reference to the "third Heaven." In Biblical times there existed a model for the universe that divided it into three layers. People could see the first two, but not the third. There are a number of theories on the meaning of the first two layers. In one theory, the first heaven refers to the sky and the second to outer space. There is a general agreement that the third heaven refers to where God, Christ, and angels dwell.

In the memory of Benja Dunning ESQ.
Who with the utmost composure,
breathed his last, Jan. 8, 1808: Æt 71
As a Husband, Parent, Christian, and
civil Magistrate, he was conspicuous.
The Town, which for many years he represented,
The Board of Overseers of Bowdoin College
and in fine civil society are deprived
of a useful, wise and peacable member.
But tho' this loss fills us with grief and pain
Our loss is his inestimable gain—For,
Thro' the eternal blue, his soul immortal,
Borne on angelic wings, at the third Heaven
Arriv'd the spirits of just men made perfect
Joined, in lofty Hallelujahs to the sacred
Triune, eternity throughout.

The following inscription on a Revolutionary War veteran's
stone is unique for the time period. It reads:

Michael Sinnett
Sep 15, 1798
æt 70
Oh wake not the hero,
his battles are o're,
Let him rest undisturbed on America's shore:
Neath this green mound of earth so flowery drest (sic),
His battles are o're let him rest,
calm rest.

Many of the epitaphs are poignant tales of early or tragic deaths.
Freeman Allen's is particularly moving.

Freeman M. Allen
Son of Elisha & Jane
March 29, 1851
æ 2y 6m
Our infant baby, the smiling boy
Its father's hope, its mother's joy
In three years resigned its breath
His sparkling eyes are boxed in death.

Joyful resurrection is the theme of Maria Johnson's 1865 epitaph. She died at age nineteen and her marble stone depicts an angel in the clouds pointing upward.

> Glad Tidings! Glad Tidings! The Kingdom is near;
> Our glorious Deliverer soon, soon will appear;
> In clouds of bright glory to our rescue he'll come,
> Angels will hail us to Heaven our Home.

Be sure to notice the monument erected to Elijah Kellogg (1813–1901), who was the first settled pastor of the Congregational Church (1843) across the street. Kellogg and his family are buried in Western Cemetery in Portland.

The vacant area near the entrance of the cemetery is the "stranger's ground" where Native Americans, slaves, transients, and the poor were buried. Burials ended when it was no longer possible to dig a new grave without unearthing an old one. There were unmarked graves throughout the cemetery. Wooden crosses that deteriorated may have been used as markers, or perhaps they were never marked.

The Old Common Cemetery serves as a tribute to the community of Harpswell for preserving their irreplaceable gravestones. The rich variety of materials and carvers, along with the easy legibility of the numerous epitaphs make this one of my favorite cemeteries to visit.

Also of Interest:

Immediately in front of the cemetery is **Harpswell's Old Meeting House**, built from 1757 to 1759 by its first pastor, Elijah Eaton and his son Samuel. This National Historic Monument is the oldest meetinghouse in the state of Maine still being used for town purposes. It retains some of the original straight-backed pews and the high pulpit, which is backed by a large multi-paned window. For more information contact the Harpswell Historical Society: *http://www.curtis library.com/hhs.htm.*

Arrowsic

NEW TOWN CEMETERY

Directions: Follow Route 1 to Woolwich. Take Route 127
south. In approximately 4.6 miles take a right onto Bald
Head Road. Go straight at the first fork and bear left at the
second fork. The cemetery will be on the right approximately
2 miles down Bald Head Road.

New Town Cemetery is a pretty woodland cemetery that is surprisingly well maintained considering that the location feels very far from anywhere. Arrowsic's population is 501, and a peek at the town hall on Route 127 verifies that Arrowsic is very small indeed. Though the cemetery is miles into the countryside, it was quite noisy the day I visited. Planes from Brunswick Naval Air Station thundered overhead, trucks rumbled over the Bath-Woolwich Bridge, and there were plenty of

Arrowsic's New Town Cemetery is small and blends well with its woodland surroundings.

crashes and crunches that I can only guess came from Bath Iron Works. A nearby target shooter reminded me it was time to wear my orange vest if I was going to be wandering around woodland cemeteries.

The graves date from the mid-18th century to the present, with the most contemporary family plot gaily decorated with red and pink plastic flowers. Most of the stones, though, are from the 1700s and 1800s. Be sure to take note of the impressive genetics implied by the number of occupants who died well into their 80s and 90s.

Arrowsic's unassuming size belies the fact that from the mid-18th century to the early 19th century this must have been a wealthy community, as there are a number of stately gravestones here. The large impressive stones of Brigadier General Samuel McCobb and Rachel McCobb seem weirdly out of place in this humble setting. His 1791 slate is embellished with a well-done winged cherub, while her stone was replaced in 1884 by her descendents.

McCobb was a Revolutionary War veteran who was in a number of battles, though the information that is most easily found is about two unsuccessful campaigns. McCobb joined Colonel Benedict Arnold on his 1775 disastrous expedition to Quebec by way of the Kennebec River. Ill equipped and ill advised, Arnold's troops were quickly weakened by starvation, disease, and the perils of Maine's wilderness. Colonel Enos and three of his companies, including Captain McCobb's, deserted several weeks into the march, taking much of the remaining food with them. McCobb makes several appearances in the fine historical novel, *Arundel*, by Kenneth Roberts. In that chronicle of the horrendous march, Enos, McCobb, and other deserting captains are portrayed as cowards for questioning the feasibility of the plan and finally for recognizing the poor odds for survival and turning back.

This was not McCobb's last adventure in defeat. As a colonel he was involved in the Penobscot Expedition of 1779, in which the British occupying Castine soundly defeated naval and infantry forces despite being greatly outnumbered.

Samuel Denny's stone (1772) is carved with two winged profiles topped by a single crown similar to the stone in Kittery. On either side of his stone are the handsome markers of his two wives, one who died in 1750 and the other in 1752.

New Town Cemetery is small, and that's including the unmarked stones that lay in the woods beyond the formal boundaries. But it is interesting due to the juxtaposition of the rustic setting with impressive gravestones and excellent carvers. The best epitaph found here is simple and lovely.

Yet all is well: God's good design I see.
That where our treasure is our heart may be.

New Town Cemetery is interesting for the juxtaposition of its rustic setting with its impressive gravestones, dating from the mid-18th century to the present.

Part Two

MID-COAST

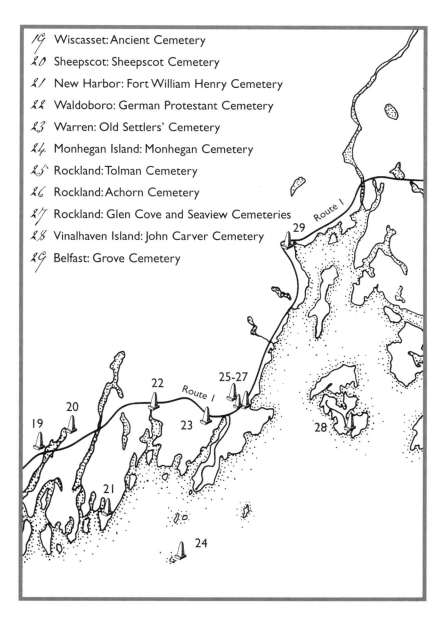

Route 1

29

25-27

22

Route 1

20

19

23

28

21

24

Wiscasset

ANCIENT CEMETERY

Directions: Follow Route 1 to Wiscasset. In the village center, turn onto Federal Street, Route 218. The cemetery is on the right, surrounded by a white picket fence.

Wiscasset claims that it is "Maine's Prettiest Village," and that may be close to the truth. Gracious homes from an earlier era flank narrow tree-lined side streets and both sides of Route 1. Water views abound from the town's perch overlooking the Sheepscot River.

The Ancient Cemetery is in the village center, on a gentle slope reaching towards the Sheepscot River. A crisp white picket fence and tidy grounds reinforce the impression that Wiscasset cares deeply about its history.

The graveyard is remarkably telling about 18th- and 19th-century life in Wiscasset, making it an anthropologist's dream. Many of the inscriptions are lengthy and without a shade of humbleness, noting the righteousness of the deceased. Virtue epitaphs abound. There is much

Located in the heart of "Maine's prettiest village," Wiscasset's Ancient Cemetery is as picturesque as the town.

more to enjoy though, than proclamations of virtue: the cemetery has the graves of sea captains, notable people, and Revolutionary War veterans, many of which feature unique carvings.

The burying ground was established in 1735 and the oldest extant stone bears the following inscription:

> Here lies the Body of
> Mr Joshua Pool
> Late of Gloster (sic)
> Aged 39 Years
> Decd June 27th
> 1739

Poor Joshua drowned when a bear capsized his canoe. The stone was re-cut and reset in 1866 out of respect for its age and the circumstances under which Joshua died.

Two stones that should not be missed belong to Manasseh Smith Esq. and Mrs. Hannah Smith. His stone is beautifully carved with a full-faced sun and the Latin inscription *Oritus occidit*, meaning "He sinks to rise." Her stone is carved with a half moon and the Latin inscription *Solem aspectat et sequitur*, meaning "She looks at and follows the sun."

An apt indication of the cultural period is reflected in their epitaphs as well. Note that the pronoun used on her stone is "they."

The unique sun and moon stones of Manasseh and Hannah Smith.

In Memory of
Manasseh Smith
Born in Leominster, Mass,
Dec 25, 1748
graduated at Harvard
College 1775; was
Chaplain in the
Revolutionary Army; Clerk
of
S. Court of Jud. Of Mass.,
settled
in this town in the practise
(sic) of

Law 1788; & declining public offices,
devoted himself to the duties of his profession,
happiness of his family & offices of piety
Died May 2, 1823

Her epitaph reads:

In Memory of
Mrs. Hannah Smith
She was the daughter of
Rev. Daniel Emerson, of Holles,
N.H., born Oct.11, 1745,
married to Manassah Smith
Feb. 17, 1774, and died his
widow, April 16, 1825
They were pious parents of
eight filial children; lived
examplars of benevolence &
Charity, & died in the Christian's
hope of a happy immortality.

Several sea captains buried here have tender and poetic epitaphs.
Captain Daniel Fagan died at age 42 in 1802. His epitaph reads:

In him
were united
those amiable qualities
which add luster
to the endearing names of Husband
Father and Friend

Captain William Baker, dead at 27 in 1813, is remembered as
follows:

Affection oft o're his sad tombstone weeps
Where a kind son, a tender husband sleeps!
A faithful mariner, generous true & just
His path the ocean, but his home the dust.
No more to roam on life's tempestuous wave
Hope's finger points to heaven while tears bedew his grave

Another young man, Captain John Patterson, died in 1810 at age twenty-six. His epitaph reads:

> Sweet are the peaceful slumber of the just
> And guardian angels watch there (sic) sacred dust
> Death is to them in richest mercy given
> To them the tomb is but the gate of heven (sic)

There are several locally well-known men buried here, but this inscription especially caught my attention:

> Ezekiel Averil
> one of Washington's body guards
> died Feb. 20, 1850 aged 95 years 8mos.

The following impassioned epitaph belonging to Deacon Nymphus Stacy is a unique testament of faith for a gravestone.

> This humble monument designates the
> spot where was deposited the mortal parts
> of Deacon Nymphus Stacy
> who died Decr. 28th A.D. 1804
> æ79
> He was not ashamed to acknowledge his divine
> Lord before men
> and the sincerity of his faith was tested by
> the habitual exercise
> of amiable dispositions, and the
> uniform practice of moral, social and
> Christian virtues. In his last moments
> he discovered firm hope in
> a glorious resurrection
> and trusting in the promise of the gospel
> he looked forward with confidence to
> the period when this
> Corruption
> Shall put on
> Incorruption
> When this mortal shall put on
> Immortality
> And death be swallowed up in
> Victory

Near the center of the cemetery is the obelisk monument to the Hon. Samuel Sewall, who was chief justice of the Supreme Court of the Commonwealth. Inscriptions cover all four sides, telling of his accomplishments and character. The north face of the stone states that his remains have been removed to the family tomb in Marblehead, Massachusetts.

Colonel Payson's gravestone is adorned with a unique rendition of a winged cherub.

Like many cemeteries in active ports, the Ancient Cemetery has an array of fine and unique carvings. In the left corner, facing the water, notice the stone of Colonel David Payson. This peculiar engraving depicts a winged cherub with what can only be described as very large breasts, though some literature claims that the period cutters were carving gourds. Over her head is a crossed trumpet and arrow, and over that is an oddly carved eye. The symbolic imagery is rich. A winged cherub is the soul's flight to heaven, the trumpet is the resurrection, the arrow is death, and the eye is the omnipresence of God, who is all knowing and all seeing. Breasts can signify divine nourishment for the soul. If they were intended as gourds, they may stand for the coming into and leaving of life or the passing away of earthly things.

On Thomas McCrate's stone is the image of a winged hourglass, standing for the swift passage of mortal time, encircled by a snake swallowing its tail, symbolizing eternity. Nathan Clark Junior's is an image of a cloudy sky, signifying the heavens, surrounding a winged globe, sometimes interpreted to mean God over all of creation.

The Ancient Cemetery presents an incredible assortment of slates, marbles, and monuments with unique inscriptions and images within a historical context. Wiscasset's history speaks through these stones in a way that is provocative and moving.

Also of Interest:

The **Castle Tucker** is an extraordinary piece of architecture that was built in 1807 by Judge Silas Lee, and remodeled in 1860 by Captain Richard H. Tucker. Besides the fascinating architecture, furnishings, and art, the guided tour also provides an inside glimpse of the life of a wealthy 19th-century sea captain. Open June 1 to October 15, Wednesday through Sunday from 11:00 to 4:00. Tours begin on the hour. Lee Street, Wiscasset. Tel: (207) 882-7364.

The **Musical Wonder House** is a most unusual museum. A guided tour allows you to see and hear an astounding number of antique music boxes, player pianos, and talking machines. Open from May 29 to October 15 daily from 10:00 to 5:00. After Labor Day, check for tour times. 18 High Street, Wiscasset. Tel: (207) 882-7163.

Just past the Ancient Cemetery is the **Lincoln County Museum and Jail**, built in 1809. Features include original prisoner graffiti, cellblocks, a kitchen exhibit, and old tools and Victoriana. Open July to Labor Day, Tuesday through Sunday from 11:00 to 4:30. 133 Federal Street, Wiscasset. Tel: (207) 882-6817.

~~Sheepscot~~
SHEEPSCOT CEMETERY

Directions: From Route 1 in Wiscasset, turn onto Federal Street, Route 218. Turn right onto Cross Road. Turn right onto King's Highway. The cemetery is on the right.

There are numerous Victorian marble gravestones in the Sheepscot Cemetery.

After following ancient directions that instructed a right turn at the village center, I missed Sheepscot three times. Whatever village center was once there is now gone. My advice for finding Sheepscot is, "Don't blink!" When I finally stumbled upon Sheepscot Cemetery, I was thoroughly impressed with its size. How can a town so small have so many dead?

The Sheepscot Cemetery is well worth the ten-minute drive from the Ancient Cemetery in Wiscasset. This inviting cemetery is surrounded by lovely countryside and sits by the Sheepscot River. It has a strong sense of place, with earth that is sturdy and solid. The layout is park-like, with rows of huge maples, scattered cedars, and woods leading down to the water. The stones date from the mid-18th century to the present, with a sampling of slates and many noteworthy Victorian marbles.

The older stones are in the familiar styles from Wiscasset, which would be expected in such proximity, but there is none of the early standout images or epitaphs to be found. What is offered are many wonderful 19th-century marbles that are in good condition and easy to read. Here is a sampling:

Thomas Cunningham
Died Jan
28 1837
Aged 82
The grave is now a favored spot
To saints who sleep in Jesus bles'd
For there the wicked trouble not
And there the weary are at rest

Anne GIiven
died Nov. 28 1828
aged 100 years
Remember thy creator
In the days of thy youth

In Memory of
Samuel Kennedy, Esq.
Who died
Octr 3, 1830 in the 82 year
of his age
Along the gentle slope of life's decline
He bent his gradual way till full of years
He dropped like mellow fruit into his grave

Elizabeth G
wife of
William Cunningham
Died
Dec. 29, 1856
Æd. 29 years
& 8 months
But still one hope the bosom cheers
By deep regret and sorrow riven
When we have passed this vale of
tears
That we shall meet again in heaven

The marble gravestone of Elizabeth Cunningham features a carved dove and garland of roses.

When you visit Sheepscot cemetery you'll want to relax under the maples and linger amid the stones. This serene and gentle cemetery will quiet your soul.

New Harbor

FORT WILLIAM HENRY CEMETERY

Directions: From Route 1 in Damariscotta, take Route 130 south to Bristol. In Bristol, turn right onto Huddle Road. In New Harbor, take the 2nd right and follow the signs to Fort William Henry.

Fort William Henry Cemetery is a privately owned cemetery that adjoins and, is maintained by, the Fort William Henry State Park. The park consists of a partially rebuilt Fort William Henry, the 1790 Fort House, and numerous archeological digs. More than 100,000 artifacts have been found, numbered, and stored to date. Johns Bay and the Pemaquid River ring the park and the cemetery with quintessential Maine harbor views of lobster boats, yachts, and summer cottages dotting a landscape of evergreens. At the tip of the point, you'll find picnic tables and a tavern offering food and drink.

Pemaquid, as this area is called, is rich in history. It was one of Maine's earliest settlements, dating back to approximately 1625. By 1670, the population had grown to around 200 people, and it was a center for the fur trade in New England. Pemaquid was England's most northern outpost and was dangerously close to France's territory. With both countries set on expansion, Pemaquid was often a battlefield. The settlements were destroyed three times by French and/or Native American attackers. It is the site of three different forts: Fort Charles, built in 1677 and destroyed in 1689; Fort William Henry, built in 1692 and destroyed in1696; and Fort Frederick, built in 1729 and probably dismantled in 1775 so that it could not be used during the Revolution by the British.

The burying ground was in use from at least 1695, when four men who were killed by Native Americans were laid to rest. The stone of Hugh March read, "H.M. 1695," and was removed for safekeeping but has since disappeared. Other graves from that period may have been marked with fieldstones or wooden crosses. The crosses have long since deteriorated, but there are many fieldstones that presumably mark graves. The oldest extant stone is from 1734 and, though the cemetery is still accepting new burials, digging of graves has become problematic. The ground must be thoroughly examined so that old unmarked graves are not unearthed. In one report, a dozen bodies were found during the digging of a single grave. Historians believe it was a mass burial following a Native American attack.

It is possible that the original cemetery was much larger than it is today. An often-repeated story tells that the owner of the Fort House had decided the cemetery was infringing on his farmland, so he ordered his men to plow through parts of it. A grave caved in under the weight of the plow, swallowing an ox. The men were then presented with the problem of getting the ox out of the hole. Not only were graves disturbed, but also household remnants from the original settlements. Unfortunately, the clearing made life difficult for present day archeologists because artifacts were moved from their original locations and spread throughout the area.

This is a small graveyard, but it presents a fascinating variety of stones, with several from the mid-18th century, including Revolutionary War veterans. The slate stones are believed to have been imported from Wales. For years it was believed that all gravestones were imported and used as ballast on ships, but no proof has ever been found. If there were imports, then they were exceptions to the rule, or it is probable they were imported prior to the 18th century. The slate has held up exceptionally well, but two Joseph Sikes stones are in poor condition, though it is still possible to read them. (See Black Point Cemetery in Scarborough for information on Joseph Sikes.) There are several carvings of winged death heads and one skull with crossbones from 1761, which is a rare treat. A 1765 stone is carved with a very sophisticated winged cherub and has visible lines that were used to write text.

The marble monuments from the 19th century are especially interesting.

One monument tells the tale of three family members who died at sea, the mother first, then the father and son. Here are their inscriptions:

Hester Maria
Wife of
Capt. Ambrose Child
Died at sea Aug. ? 1850
Aged 39 years
Far from home her life had blest

The gentle ? found her rest
Seek ye her epitaph is traced
On heart and ne'r can be effaced

Capt.
Ambrose Child
Died 1862
Æ 43 years
Safe from ocean's heaving billows
Life's rough voyage with thee is oer,
On the Savior's bosom pillowed;
Thou will rest forever more.

Alexr M. Child
Died 1862
Æ 17 years
Thy mother sleeps beneath this mound
Thou in an ocean grave
Their spirits mingle round the throne
Their severed from their graves

When the parking lot was being dug, the skeletal remains of a Native American were found, and in the 1960s several others were found. All of the remains were returned to the appropriate Native American tribe. It's unfortunate that a monument has not been erected to honor the Native Americans who also shared in the land and history of Pemaquid.

Fort William Henry Cemetery is thoroughly engrossing. Perhaps it is because of the proximity of the historic fort and house, or the variety of early stone carvers, or even its beautiful view. All these features combine to create a remarkable place.

Dating back to at least 1695, the Fort William Henry Cemetery has a wide variety of markers and beautiful water views.

Also of Interest:

Plan on spending time investigating **Colonial Pemaquid**, which includes Fort William Henry and the Fort House. The fort was one of the earliest stone forts in the United States. The French destroyed it four years after it was built, dashing the belief that it was impregnable. There is a small museum, and on the grounds, markers help to make sense of the fort foundations, former barracks, and excavations. Open daily May 31 to Labor Day, from 9:30 to 5:30. Colonial Pemaquid, New Harbor. Tel: (207) 677-2423.

Waldoboro
GERMAN PROTESTANT CEMETERY

Directions: From Route 1 in Waldoboro, turn onto Route 32 south. The cemetery will be on the right, south of the village.

The personality of the German Protestant Cemetery is very distinctive and unique. The long slender burial ground is entered through a wrought-iron archway. A beautifully preserved meetinghouse sits at the base of a slope that is crowded with 19th-century graves and monuments. There are vacant places to be found, but it's safe to assume that they hold unmarked graves. Burials still occur here, though the new section is in the back so that nothing mars the beauty of the hillside filled with marble in varying shades of white and bordered with massive shade trees. If you listen carefully, you can hear the brook along the left side. The mossy ground is heavily mounded with graves, and it must have taken special effort on the part of gravediggers to prevent erosion from washing away the hillside and exposing the caskets.

The history of those buried here, and of their ancestors who populate the many small graveyards of the area, is rich in forbearance, determination, and struggle. Even the strongest and the most courageous settlers could not always survive the circumstances of Waldoboro's early years.

A beautifully preserved meetinghouse sits at the base of the German Protestant Cemetery in Waldoboro.

Their story begins in 1731, when Samuel Waldo of Boston traveled to England to represent thirty men who owned the land that later became known as Waldo and Knox counties. Waldo was able to support their claim and in return they rewarded him with part of the land. Subsequently, Waldo came to own the entire parcel, which became known as the Waldo Patent.

Waldo had a vision of creating a thriving and well-populated community, so he sent his son Samuel Jr. to Germany to recruit settlers. Germany was probably chosen because of the high level of skilled workers to be found there; Waldo was after tradesmen who could transform his wilderness. Early records seem to indicate that the first settlement of German immigrants arrived sometime between 1739 and 1742. By 1746, they had been completely decimated by Native American attacks and the harsh New England elements. It is speculated that some of them joined Waldo on William Pepperell's expedition to Louisburg in 1745 and never returned to the area.

Between 1748 and 1752, Waldo convinced approximately seventy to eighty more Germans to settle Waldoboro. Then, in another effort, he circulated flyers advertising for 120 families. The flyers promoted Waldoboro as a populous town and promised an array of benefits to those who signed on. His brochure offered 120 acres of land, fronting a navigable river, that would be deeded over, no payment due, to families who stayed on the land for seven years. A school, church, and minister would receive two hundred acres each upon establishment. Families were to be provided with six months of supplies and all the tools they needed for homesteading. They were assured that they would receive religious protection, exemption from military service, and a deputy to represent them in court. Waldo failed to make clear that they would be traveling to a Spartan wilderness of harsh winters and an ongoing war between Native Americans and settlers; but worse than that, they were unaware that they would become indentured servants for four to six years to repay their transportation to Waldoboro.

Sixty families arrived in September 1753 with little time to prepare for winter. The fortunate families were invited to board with those few who already had established homes. The rest lodged in a sixty-foot-long shed not fit for human habitation. Seventeen died from starvation and exposure that first winter.

It is difficult to imagine the grueling hardship and poverty of those early years. The settlers had no knowledge of living in the wilderness and were not skilled in hunting and fishing. Most survived on clams.

Out of desperation, children and wives were put out to service in the Saint George and Damariscotta areas. In addition, they were subject to random attacks by Native Americans.

Waldo's representative, who was suspected of pocketing a profit, sold the supplies that were supposed to be free. As far as promised equipment went—each family was given a crude hoe. Not a single family was ever granted ownership of the property to which they were rightfully entitled, unless they purchased it. First, the settlers of Waldoboro had to buy their freedom, and then they had to buy their land.

The 1760s bought peace to New England and an influx of settlers to Waldoboro who were predominantly middle class and well educated. Life became easier as mills, shipyards, and roads were built. In 1773, Waldoboro was incorporated and rapidly prospered through the 1800s. By the Civil War, Waldoboro was the largest settlement in the area, with shipbuilding dominating the riverfront, but there were also wool mills, a button factory, and quarry work.

Once their basic needs were met, the German population could focus their attention on religion. The 1772 meetinghouse at the entrance of the cemetery is one of the three oldest in the state and the earliest Lutheran one. In 1795, the meetinghouse was dismantled and moved to its present location on the "ministerial lot" promised by Waldo. The oldest headstone is dated 1797, but burials probably occurred prior to that time. While exploring the cemetery it is useful to know that the German names were Anglicized upon their arrival. The English kept the records and spelled the names as they sounded.

Near the top of the hill is an obelisk inscribed on three sides. One side tells the story of the early immigrants, while the other sides honor two early Lutheran ministers: Reverend Augustus Rodolphus Benedectus Ritz (yes, that is a single name.) and Reverend John William Starman. Reverend Ritz arrived in Waldoboro in 1794 and was the first settled minister and the first to preach from the meetinghouse in its present location. Reverend Starman gave his first sermon in 1812. Convinced that it was important for the Germans to speak English, he worked hard to learn the language. From 1820 to 1835, on one Sunday a month he gave his sermon in English.

Next to this obelisk is a monument marking the grave of Conrad Heyer, who was the first child born in the 1748 settlement. Heyer's inscription reads:

Conrad Heyer
Born
April 10, 1749
Died
Feb. 19, 1856
Aged 106 yrs.
10 mos. 9 days.

According to his marker, he lived 106 years, but according to math, he lived 105. This has been much commented on, though no satisfactory explanation has been found. At that age, why dicker over a year? Referred to as Old Waldoborough's first citizen, "Mr. H.'s" life spanned two centuries and witnessed incredible changes and challenges, starting with the death of his father from starvation just before his birth. He was well known, well liked, and admired by many as can be attested to by his funeral service. The Bath *Daily Tribune* printed a lengthy account of the ceremony that was reprinted in *Waldoborough 200 Anniversary Pictorial History*. On June 17, 1856, his body was exhumed from where it had been buried since his death and re-interred with elaborate ceremony in its present place of honor. According to the Bath *Daily Tribune* article, the day began in the village center at 11:00 A.M. where a procession of approximately four thousand people gathered. The large number of people who attended can be attributed to his great age, his popularity, and especially to his high status as a Revolutionary War veteran. Two military guard units escorted the procession: the Conrad Guards and the Rockland City Guards led by the Mayor of Rockland, Captain H.G. Berry. (Berry has a monument in Achorn Cemetery in Rockland.) The Rockland Band and the Bath Cornet Band provided music.

Before the procession went to the cemetery, there was a light lunch for invited guests at the hall on the corner of Main and Water streets. After this collation, the coffin was opened so that the body could be viewed. According to the day's account, many people commented on how preserved he still looked, with barely any discoloration. The next stop was the meetinghouse, where prayers, hymns, and eulogies were given in his honor. The eulogies spoke of his industriousness, patriotism, and religious faith. There was reminiscing about his Revolutionary War stories that he told so well.

The daylong event continued into the evening. At 5:00 P.M. two hundred people sat down to enjoy dinner, entertainment, and music.

The un-cited author of the article fairly gushed with his pleasure at the day and was very pleased to note that there was not a single occurrence of drunkenness.

There are many interesting epitaphs here, with most from the mid-19th century, though one of my favorites is from 1798. It reads:

In Memory of
Mary Elenor Levensyler
Wife of
John Adam Levensyler
died Decr. 19th 1798
Aged 66 Years
Invisible am I
To this blind world below.

A marble headstone carved with a wreath encircling a book inscribed "Thy Memory Lives," is a lovely stone with the following inscription:

Capt
Thos Creamer
Died
Aug. 21, 1858
Æ 55 y's 5ms.
O weep not for me for my spirit has fled,
To mansions of rest in the sky
The friend you have loved is not sleeping and dead
But gone to his father on high.

The vision of the meetinghouse backed by a gathering of headstones and memorials acts as a symbolic representation of the unity and closeness this settlement of German immigrants felt. The German Protestant Cemetery has interesting stones, a definite personality, and a rich heritage.

Also of Interest:

After Samuel Waldo died, the Waldo Patent was divided between his four children, Samuel Jr., Francis, Lucy, and Hannah. Hannah married Thomas Flucker, who purchased Samuel's share. Lucy died without children, and Francis and Thomas both had to forfeit their land after the Revolution because they were Tories. Henry Knox married Flucker's daughter and purchased ⅘ of the patent, while his wife owned the other ⅕, making Knox the owner of the entire parcel. In 1793, Henry Knox, who was a major general in the Revolutionary War and the nation's first secretary of war, built his mansion **Montpelier**, which was modeled upon George Washington's Mount Vernon. Knox's dream of recreating a grand country estate did not work out as he had hoped, for the home was not designed for harsh Maine winters. The current building is actually a faithful reproduction of the original and is decorated with some of Knox's furnishings. It features an oval front room, a butterfly staircase, and many fine period details. Open Memorial Day to Labor Day, Tuesday through Sunday from 10:00 to 4:00. Route 1, Thomaston. Tel: (207) 354-8062.

The elaborately carved stones of Elbridge and Esther Parker. His features Masonic symbols and hers an open book and drapery.

Warren

OLD SETTLERS' CEMETERY

Directions: From Route 1 in Warren, turn onto Old Settler's Road, which is 2.3 miles north of the intersection of Route 1 and Route 90. Park at the top of the street and walk in. At the end of the street, follow the wide trail that heads straight back into the woods. Follow the trail for approximately 1/4 mile.

Erected in 1913, the granite monument bears the names of the first settlers to arrive in Warren in 1736.

I'm always grateful for happy coincidences that lead me to cemeteries I might have missed. In this case, I was led to Old Settlers' Cemetery by a chance conversation with a Rockland librarian who had done graduate work on early gravestone carvings. No doubt you, too, will meet people along this tour who will tell you of their favorite graveyards and point you in a direction that I didn't take, which is a large part of the fun.

When all of the gravestones come from a short historic time period, visiting the burial ground is like being transported back in time. The Old Settlers' Cemetery is such a place. Unlike Arrowsic, with its bellowing noises of technology and newer graves, here there are only the sounds of nature and graves that date from 1736 to 1792. Imagine the fern-lined path to be an early road leading down to the Oyster River, which is less than fifty yards away from the cemetery. Between the river and the cemetery was the First Presbyterian Church. Along the Oyster and Saint George rivers, forty-eight lots were carved out, and this area came to be known as the upper settlement. Etched onto the monument erected in 1913 are the names of the first settlers who arrived here in 1736 ready to farm their lots.

Except for the 20th-century monument and flagpole, the cemetery may look as it did more than two hundred years ago. It is roughly cleared, save for a few large oaks. It is only mowed occasionally, so small shrubs, brush, and various groundcovers compete with the gravestones for space. The uneven ground speaks of the unmarked graves, while fieldstones and uncarved slabs mark others. There are a few large well-carved stones, more mid-sized modest stones, and many humble markers allowing for judgments about the financial status of the earliest settlers.

There is an eclectic mix of stonecutters as well. One man whose work is found throughout the Rockland area can be recognized by his skeleton heads that resemble childish ghosts more than frightening death heads. A handmade stone is roughly carved 1774, while the elegant slates of John Boggs and Captain Thomas Kilpatrick dominate the burial ground.

John Boggs's stone is in the rear corner and is well carved but poorly repaired. His 1773 epitaph is a version of the ever popular "Stop here Friend and Cast an Eye . . ." Boggs originally settled here in 1736, but left to bring his family to Boston from 1745 to 1749 when the settlement was nearly abandoned due to attacks by French and Native Americans. Settlers throughout the region had hoped that the defeat of the French in Louisburg would bring peace at last, but it only further incited those tribes that had formed affiliations with the French. In 1748, Louisburg was returned to France and the fifth of six French and Indian Wars was concluded. Those who chose to return found that their settlement had been destroyed. Boggs started anew and became a successful farmer while running an alewife fishery. In *The Annals of Warren*, Cyrus Eaton writes that Boggs was forced from Ireland as a consequence of his battles with the Roman Catholic Irish, whom he loathed. But America failed to deliver him from his archenemies. While in Philadelphia, his daughter fell in love with an Irish Catholic and married him despite her father's condemnation. Her mother managed to send her linens as a dowry, but her father disowned her.

The impressive stone close to the path belongs to another early settler, Captain Thomas Kilpatrick, who passed in 1772. Upon returning to the settlement in 1749, Kilpatrick reorganized the militia and was elected captain. According to Eaton, Kilpatrick was considered a terror to the Native Americans and was referred to as "Tom-Kill-the-Devil" by Governor Pownal.

Directly in front of, and facing, Kilpatrick's stone is James Lemond's, who died at the age of seventeen from a fever that moved along the river, leaving many dead in 1771 and 1772.

Towards the left side is the large rectangular gravestone of a woman who faced many trials. It is inscribed as follows:

Isabella A Gamble
Wife of D. 1779
A.G.
D. 1783

Often it is difficult, if not impossible, to find information about women settlers. Warren's monument to the first settlers is a case in point; only men are listed, though it is known that women arrived with them. In *The Annals of Warren*, women are listed only by their surname, making exact identity difficult. Luckily, Isabella Gamble's story was too interesting for historians to ignore. From *The Annals of Warren* we learn that in 1740 Native Americans brought word to Warren of shipwreck survivors on Mount Desert Island. The *Grand Design* was carrying wealthy Irish passengers and their bonded servants who were intending to join colonists in Pennsylvania when a storm drove the ship ashore. After the shipwreck, a group of one hundred set off in hopes of finding a settlement. They were never heard from again. Isabella was then the newlywed Mrs. Galloway and was accompanied by her husband and their three-month-old nursing son.

Months passed, supplies from the ship had run out, and the group that stayed behind was near death. Her husband traded two pieces of linen for a duck from a Native American, and then declined to eat it so that she and the baby would have nourishment. Surely he sacrificed his own life, for he soon died. Meanwhile, Isabella became close friends with an un-named woman who was a newlywed and whose husband died at the same time. Together they dug graves for their spouses.

Soon after, the group was rescued and brought back to Warren, where Isabella and her friend were relieved to find an Irish settlement that was hospitable and understood their language. Within a short time, Archibald Gamble, a young Irish colonist with a farm in the upper settlement, asked for her hand in marriage, and likewise another settler, Mr. McCarter, asked her friend the same. Both women accepted the proposals and remained close friends until their deaths.

Isabella's decision to quickly remarry so infuriated her former brother-in-law that he sent for the child, who Isabella refused to give up, claiming that her son would decide on his own when he was older. He was later lost at sea.

In 1757, Isabella Gamble again appears in *The Annals of Warren*. While en route to New Hampshire to spend her pregnancy with a relative, her vessel was attacked by French and Native Americans. Through a series of events, Isabella and an older man were the only two left on board. Keeping careful watch, they spotted attackers approaching the ship under cover of the night. Isabella and the man successfully defended themselves by the man shooting muskets that she quickly reloaded. Their lives were sparred, but Isabella miscarried that morning.

Isabella's challenges continued when she lost her husband. He was hauling hay across the frozen river when he fell through the ice and drowned.

The benign neglect, the rustic setting, the abundance of humbly marked graves, along with the sense of being transported back in time, make for a haunting aura in the Old Settlers' Cemetery. I'm grateful for the chance conversation that brought me here and for the opportunity to reflect on life in another era.

A primitively carved slate stone
from the Old Settlers' Cemetery.

Monhegan Island
MONHEGAN CEMETERY

Directions: From Route 1 in Thomaston, turn onto Route 131 south and follow to Port Clyde. Take the one-hour ferry from Port Clyde to Monhegan Island. Reservations for the ferry are strongly suggested. (Telephone: 207-372-8848.) On the island the cemetery can be easily spotted uphill from the village center or just downhill from the lighthouse.

Beautiful Mohegan Island. Headlands crashing into the sea, fishhouses edging to the water, a beach filled with dinosaur-egg-rocks, a pine forest dotted with fairy houses, meandering trails filled with scents from both the ocean and the earthy forest, and air so abundant and crystalline that it makes the lungs rejoice. We live in a time when strip malls and chain stores erase the differences between places, and everywhere begins to look like everywhere else. Monhegan is different. It is its own unique place with a wonderfully strong sense of self.

Monhegan's cemetery overlooks the village from its spot on the hill just below the lighthouse.

Monhegan's history began four thousand years ago when the Stone Age Red Paint People fished its waters and enjoyed their catch around campfires. For centuries, Native Americans rowed twelve miles out to sea to take advantage of the fishing. Norsemen may have visited a thousand years ago. John Smith, the tireless English explorer and promoter of New England, came to Monhegan in 1614 with forty-five men and boys and planted crops that were used to sustain the struggling colonists at Plymouth Plantation.

Monhegan was an active English settlement until 1675, when the Anglo-Abenaki War or King Phillip's War broke out. It was the first in a series of six wars that would last until 1763, when the Treaty of Paris was signed. It is believed that the war was ignited when the Abenaki burned coastal settlements in retaliation for the deliberate drowning of Chief Squando's child by English sailors. Monhegan residents responded with vengeance by offering five pounds for every Native American scalp brought in. As coastal settlements burned, more than three hundred colonists arrived on Monhegan seeking shelter. The swelled population quickly depleted the island's resources. Faced with starvation, the settlers petitioned Massachusetts, and a rescue ship was sent. The three-year war is estimated to have killed or driven away six thousand settlers along the coast.

Monhegan remained unsettled until Henry Trefethren, of Kittery, purchased the island in 1790 and sent his children, Mary, Sarah, and Henry Jr., with their spouses, to live there. This is where the tale of Monhegan Cemetery begins. As you roam through the burial ground you will become familiar with these names. Henry Trefethren Jr. married Jemina Starling. Jemina's brother Josiah married Mary, and Sarah married Thomas Horn. To avoid confusion in the cemetery, it is important to know that these surnames were later changed to Trefethern, Sterling, and Orne. The three families divided the island equally and lived communally. Together they created the foundation for the island's culture as it exists today. Of the seventy-five full-time residents presently living on the island, several can trace their bloodlines back to the original three families. One of those people is Zoe Zanidakis, who was a contestant on the *Survivor IV* television show.

We owe a debt of gratitude to the Trefethrens for their belief that no one should be denied access to the island's beauty. To this day, seventeen miles of trails, many that cross private property, are open to the public.

The cemetery sits firmly planted into the side of Monhegan's highest point at 178 feet above sea level. It is just below the lighthouse and just above the village, and it commands breathtaking views of nearby Manana Island and the sea beyond. It is a relatively small cemetery with approximately one hundred and twenty markers and several unmarked areas that appear to hold graves.

The earliest gravestones are the two small slates that mark the deaths of Mary and Josiah Starling's infant daughters: Phebe in 1784 and Mary in 1790. Fortunately, they had eleven more children, six of whom remained on the island. The scratched-out date, uncentered wording, and varying scripts may mark Mary's stone as the work of an inexperienced cutter.

Josiah, who was a Revolutionary War veteran, passed away in 1832 and his epitaph is the classic "Remember me as you pass by. . ." In the Monhegan Historical

One of Monhegan's earliest graves is that of two-year-old Mary Starling.

and Cultural Museum, a Tower musket belonging to Josiah is on exhibit. The story behind the gun is that Josiah sailed out to the English ship *Boxer* to ask the ship's doctor if he would come ashore and assist his crippled son. The doctor agreed, and he and several shipmen spent the night at Josiah's. The following morning the men heard blasts coming from Pemaquid and raced out to the cemetery where they could see that the Boxer was under attack. In order to make haste back to their ship, the men traded their weapons for a boat. The 1813 battle was between the *Boxer* and the American *Enterprise*. The brig *Enterprise* won the day, but both sea captains were killed and are buried side by side in Eastern Cemetery in Portland. (See Eastern Cemetery for more information.)

Josiah Starling Jr. followed in his father's footsteps to become a prominent fisherman. He eventually became a successful Yankee trader who sailed the coast of Maine and Massachusetts with his two-masted schooners. At the time of his death, he left his five children $10,000 each, a sizable fortune in the mid-nineteenth century.

Buried here is Sarah E. Albee, who is largely responsible for attracting rusticators and artists to Monhegan. Starting in the 1870s, artists became captivated by Monhegan's natural beauty. Early on they were small in number and hosted by island families. Sarah, who was widowed with two small boys, saw an opportunity. In 1875, Sarah opened her home as a boarding house. That house, which is still standing, was *The Influence*, built in 1826 by Henry and Ann Trefethren. She was so successful that in 1890 she opened the island's first hotel. As proprietor of the Albee House, presently the Monhegan House, Sarah promoted Monhegan as a summer resort. She managed the hotel for twenty years before passing away at age seventy-three. Part of her legacy is the long list of artists that enjoyed her hospitality and those who continued to visit the island after her death. A short list includes such famous artists as George Bellows, James Fitzgerald, Mary Titcomb, Rockwell Kent, Robert Henri, Edward Hopper, N.C. Wyeth, Andrew Wyeth, and Jamie Wyeth.

It is surprising that in a village community surrounded by the sea that there is not a single legible epitaph that refers to the ocean or to death at sea. Reuben Davis drowned in 1905, but only a Free Mason insignia adorns his simple stone.

Reuben's story lends insight into life and death on Monhegan. In the mid-afternoon he went out to clear a lobster pot and somehow his skiff went down. Reuben's attempt to swim ashore was foiled by his heavy oil clothes and the long rubber boots that pulled him to the bottom thirty feet from shore. When his body was found, he was standing straight with his arms floating high above his head. In *Maine Memories*, by Elizabeth Coatsworth, a story is recounted of how his wife rowed out to where he was last seen alive and made an offering to the ocean of his Bible, his slippers and even his cat tied in a sack.

Squire Davis, as he was called, was a well-liked and valuable man on the island. His family arrived here just after the War of 1812, along with the Wincapaws and Pierces. He was one of the last fishermen to wear gold earrings for good luck. His obituary described him as ". . . a man of large heart, generous and upright in all his dealings." Seventy-five Masons, mostly from the mainland, and the entire island population attended his funeral. The Masons performed his last rites and, clad in white aprons and gloves, they carried Reuben to his hillside grave.

The strong imagery of the island's burials is rendered in James Fitzgerald's watercolor of Walter Davis' funeral. In the painting, chilling wind and rain accost the funeral procession of bent figures, many

Many gravestones in Monhegan Cemetery bear the name Davis.

dressed in yellow oil clothes, as they wind their way through the village carrying the casket. It is titled *Island Funeral*, and is printed in *Monhegan: The Artists' Island*, along with other incredible works of art.

Elizabeth Coatsworth also tells of a grandmother who passed away and there was no wood available to build a coffin. According to the story, her granddaughter could not help but giggle at the funeral when she envisioned her grandmother going off to heaven in a canvas topsail.

There are a number of legible epitaphs and with the cemetery still in use, it is interesting to trace the families through time. Start with Mary Starling, an original settler and Daughter of the American Revolution.

Mary
Widow of
Josiah Starling
Aged 74 years
They die in jesus (sic) and are blest
How sweet their slumbers are

The following epitaph from 1877 is not entirely legible, but can be found in its entirety in the Monhegan Historical and Cultural Museum Association records.

Asleep in Jesus would ye break

The calm which heaven pronounces blessed
And to a world of tears awake
Those who in death's soft slumber rest
Why should we wish that those we love
Should share the tears and woes we feel
Why should our hearts with sorrow move
Their tearless eyelids to unseal
Weep for yourselves whose weary feet
Must still earth's shorny pathway tread
Weep not for me whose rest is sweet
Among the safe the blessed dead.

The temptation on Monhegan is not to read the epitaphs at all, but to quietly settle onto a bench at the lighthouse, contemplate life on Monhegan and watch the sunset on the cemetery and the sea.

Also of Interest:

The **Monhegan Historical and Cultural Museum** includes the island's historical archives, an art gallery, and a museum featuring exhibits on local history, botanical life, and geography. Open July 1 through August. At the Lighthouse. Call for hours. Tel: (207) 596-7003.

The temptation on Monhegan is not to read the epitaphs at all, but to simply take pleasure in the place.

Rockland

TOLMAN CEMETERY

***Directions:** From Route 1 in downtown Rockland, turn onto Route 17 west. Turn left onto Old County Road after 1.1 miles. Take an immediate right onto Lake Avenue. The cemetery is approximately .4 mile on the right.*

Rockland, in the heart of the Penobscot Bay area, is a commercial port famous for its lobster industry. The downtown district maintains much of its architectural integrity and by touring this bustling town, you can experience the mark left by a history of shipbuilding, quarrying, and commercial fishing.

With stones dating back to 1783, Tolman Cemetery is Rockland's oldest.

The town's first settlers came to rest in Tolman Cemetery. It's perched on a knoll overlooking rolling fields and wooded hills, and sparkling birches dot the grounds, which are bordered by old maples and oaks. The stone wall along one side was commissioned in 1810 for $50 and was completed by Jacob Ulmer. If you peek through the back trees you'll see Chickawaukie Pond.

Tolman Cemetery is Rockland's oldest graveyard, with stones dating from the late 18th century to the mid-19th century. In 1783, Isaiah Tolman donated one acre of his land for use as a cemetery. Isaiah and his family arrived here between 1765 and 1769, making them the first known settlers of Shore Village, which was part of Thomaston until 1850, when Rockland was incorporated. Isaiah was widowed twice and married three times. His three wives bore twenty-one children, seventeen of whom survived. He built a sawmill that became the center of the community and, with his wives, he was largely responsible for populating and building early Rockland. Ironically, Isaiah is not buried in Tolman Cemetery, though many of his kin are. He and his third wife retired to Matinicus, where they are buried.

In the 1770s, Shore Village was still a remote, untamed wilderness, but the French and Indian Wars were over and settlers began once again to populate the shores of Maine. During this period, twelve families came to Shore Village, and their names are found in Tolman and throughout Rockland's cemeteries: Spear, Reed, Linsey, Holmes, Spofford, Barrows, Fales, Keen, Blackington, Killsa, Rankin, and Crockett. The Ulmers and Achorns soon followed.

Most of Rockland's Revolutionary War veterans are buried here. A plaque at the entrance states:

> Tolman Cemetery
> To Honor and Commemorate Those
> Men of the Army and Navy Who Bore
> Arms in the American Revolution
> and Who Fostered True Patriotism
> in Preserving Love of Country
> and Securing for Mankind All
> the Blessings of Liberty
> (Twenty-one names are listed.)
> Erected by the Maine Society
> Daughters of the American Revolution
> July 25, 1947

It should be noted that from their inception at the turn of the 20th century, the Daughters of the American Revolution were very active in preserving Tolman Cemetery.

Several Tolmans, who are named on the plaque, have graves in the cemetery. Other listed veterans who were from the original twelve families of Shore Village are Spear, Fales, Keen, Blackington, and Killsa.

The beautiful slate headstones, veined with quartz, are common to this area and makes only rare appearances elsewhere in the state. The gravestones carved from this slate are very dark with white and gray swirls, and are usually cut in simple rectangles with shallow carving due to the slate's hardness. It appears that the slate markers that contain more quartz have rounded tops and deeper carving. Tolman Cemetery has more of this type of slate than any of the other cemeteries listed here. Several stones are carved with the ghost-like death heads also found in Warren. There are fieldstones serving as markers,

A traditional death head from a gravestone at Tolman Cemetery.

traditional death heads, and many, many willow and urn motifs.

It is not unusual to find markers for multiple children who all died within a short time span, and Tolman Cemetery is no exception. Here we find six small headstones from the same family. Five children under the age of ten died from August 15 through September 7, in 1792. There are five identical stones and set off from the others, a sixth more humble stone simply engraved, "B.J." It seems safe to surmise that this is a sixth dead child. The parents do not appear to be buried here. Some contagion—possibly diphtheria—spread through the area in the 1790s, followed by smallpox in 1800. Perhaps these account for the large number of young people buried here.

There are some good epitaphs, and a few are quite original, as in the following inscription dating from 1848:

> I have fought a good fight, I have
> finished my course, I have kept
> the path

The following epitaph is from 1839:

> O' Mother dear how hard to part
> With you our earliest love;
> But God has called you from us,
> To dwell in heaven above.

Due to its small size, you won't need to linger long at Tolman Cemetery, but the unusual slate, the graves of American Revolution veterans, and its pretty setting makes it a worthwhile stop.

Also of Interest:

The **Farnsworth Museum** is one of Maine's best museums, and the only one that focuses on Maine's role in American art. The museum also features the **Wyeth Center**, which opened in 1998 and presents three generations of Wyeth painters. Open year round. Memorial Day through Columbus Day from 9:00 to 5:00 daily. Off-season from 10:00 to 5:00 Tuesday through Saturday. Sunday from 1:00 to 5:00. 356 Main Street (Route 1), Rockland. Tel: (207) 596-6457. *www.farnsworth museum.org.*

This 1792 slate gravestone is for an eight-year-old boy—one of the many children who died in the late 18th century and are buried at Tolman Cemetery.

Rockland

ACHORN CEMETERY

Directions: From Route 1 in downtown Rockland, turn onto Route 17 west. Turn left onto Old County Road after 1.1 miles. Take an immediate right onto Lake Avenue. The cemetery entrance is a quick left at the yellow fire hydrant.

Achorn Cemetery is large and sprawling, reflecting the prosperity of 19th-century Rockland.

If Tolman Cemetery represents Rockland as an early settlement, then the Achorn Cemetery moves to the next generation that lived in the prosperous mid- to late-19th century. It is a large cemetery of nearly 2,400 lots and the potential for more than 15,000 graves. Acres and acres of marble, limestone, and occasionally granite headstones are framed by Rockland's rolling hills. Hours can be spent reading epitaphs, examining carvings, and finding the graves of notable people. The contemporary section is small, but an excellent reflection of present-day marker trends and evolving graveside customs.

Upon entering, pass under an arch that claims, "The Dead Shall Be Raised," and follow the main avenue across the front of the cemetery. On your left are the Bird and Smith family plots with their outsized obelisks. The color change and the construction of the Smith monument makes it look as if it was actually made taller at one point. Were

This massive obelisk marks the plot of the Smith family.

the Smiths in competition with the Birds in death as in life? Also note the Cremains Garden around the flagpole, with its flush ground markers.

The third monument and family plot belongs to the Cobb family. Francis Cobb arrived in Shore Village in 1818 and quickly became a prominent businessman involved in lime quarrying, shipbuilding, and banking. His company is the source of the gravestones that are found throughout the state marked, "F. Cobb & Co." in the lower right corners. By 1885, he annually produced half a million casks of lime and owned the forty ships necessary to carry the lime to market. In 1890, Francis' son William (1857–1937) took over the family business, which he continued to expand until, in 1904, he was nominated as the Republican candidate for governor and voted into office. After serving four years, he returned to private life and according to *Shore Village Story, An Informal History of Rockland Maine*, at the time of his retirement he was president of Eastern Steamlines Inc., The Androscoggin Electric Company, Bath Iron Works, and the Camden and Rockland Water Company.

Continuing around to the back avenue, notice the unusual faux wood crucifix marker belonging to Octave Howard, who died in 1922. It is reminiscent of Athearn's carvings on Vinalhaven, though not as skilled.

The large tomb made from native granite belongs to one of

The tomb of Union general Davis Tillson is constructed of native granite.

Rockland's most renowned citizens. Davis Tillson (1830–1895) rose to the rank of brigadier general in the Union Army, despite a foot amputation that prevented him from graduating from West Point. In 1861, he organized the 2nd Maine Artillery Battery. In May of 1862, he was promoted to major and participated in the Battles of Cedar Mountain, Second Bull Run, and Rappahanock Station. He was commissioned brigadier general in 1863 and appointed chief of artillery for the Department of Ohio. As a general, he successfully petitioned for permission to organize the first African-American troops for the U.S. Heavy Artillery. He stayed in the army after the war and directed the Freedmen's Bureau of Tennessee and Georgia, which managed all matters relating to freed persons, including marriage records, labor contracts, government rations, back pay, relief, educational activities, and supervision of abandoned or confiscated Confederate lands.

After returning to civilian life, Tillson successfully speculated in many areas: he engaged in the cotton business, opened a lime quarry, purchased an orange grove, and built a $100,000 wharf in Rockland. Many predicted the wharf would be his financial ruin, but again the risk brought him wealth. He died at age sixty-five from heart disease.

Of special note along the back of the cemetery is the veteran's section. The cemetery has a total of seventy-two veterans and forty-five of them are buried in this section. The government-issue markers range from the Civil War through World War II.

Turning back towards the entrance, choose the road that will take you to the statue of Hiram Berry, another notable Civil War veteran. Berry's youthful ambitions to become a military man were firmly discouraged by his parents. He found a place in politics as a State Representative in 1852 and then as Mayor of the newly formed

Rockland in 1856. He also started a
company that manufactured sashes,
blinds, and doors, but at the start of
the Civil War he followed his childhood dream and promptly enlisted in
the 4th Maine Volunteer Infantry. He
was engaged in the First Battle of Bull
Run and the Seige of Yorktown, and in
1862 was made major general of the
U.S. Volunteers. In the Battle of
Chancellorsville, Berry led several bayonet charges, but was mortally wounded by enemy fire while delivering
orders to his men.

Moving to the next avenue
towards the center, five plots down on
the left is the Ulmer family, where
there are two Civil War and one War
of 1812 veterans buried. Ulmer is a
name found throughout the cemetery,
as it was the Ulmers and the Birds
who established the cemetery, though
a portion of it was originally the
Achorn family burial ground. William
Ulmer's inscription follows:

*A statue marks the grave of another Civil
War veteran and Rockland's first mayor:
General Hiram Berry.*

Gen. William
Ulmer
Died May 4, 1845
Aged 31 years
8 months &
19 days
Thou art in the grave, my Husband lay thy
sickness wasted frame,
And thy loved ones call, ah! vainly on thy
loved and cherished name:
Thy form alone is all, Thank God! That to the
grave is given,
For we know thy soul, thy better part is safe
yes, safe in Heaven.

The following epitaph is a good representation of the epitaphs found here. It belongs to Amanda Norton, who died in 1858.

> Although my mortal frame is laid
> Beneath the church yard's lonely sod,
> The debt was due, it now is paid
> And I'm a king and priest to God
> My sleep how calm Ò my peace how pure
> The world no more can me molest;
> Though dead to friends, my soul survives
> In faith's unclouded clime of rest.

In the new section, some gravesites that are embellished with religious icons, decorations, toys, and chimes serve as altars to the deceased. A granite marker is etched with the sun rising over the ocean and is inscribed:

> Nicholas Frank
> Feb.12, 1991
> June 11, 1999
> You light up my life.
> We Love You
> Our Angel

A butterfly bush, flowers, an autumn pumpkin and a tickling wind chime have turned the lot into a garden. A closer look reveals an action-figure doll, model cars, a small golf club, a pinwheel and special beach rocks.

There are a number of granite markers that have photographs of the deceased attached to the front. Jeffrey Keene Kelly (1952-2000) was a disabled Vietnam veteran, and the lengthy inscriptions on the front and back of his stone are a testament of love from his wife.

There appears to be a renewed interest in leaving messages that offer clues to the person's identity. Edward Coffin's stone states:

> Born Nantucket Is.
> Land Surveying, Boats,
> Airplanes & Books
> Consumed My Life, With
> Diana, Jeffrey & My Wives
> August 10, 1923–

Barbara Coffin's inscription reads:

Family, Tennis, Sunshine,
Were Her Life.
MAR. 26, 1925 MAR. 30, 1977

Achorn Cemetery, along with Seaview and Tolman, are beautifully maintained and preserved by the Rockland Cemetery Association. The association was established in the early 1900s and incorporated in 1917. Their success and solvency is attributed to the longevity of the presidents, trustees, and employees; since incorporation there have been only three presidents. The association employs a full-time superintendent and a seasonal crew of four. Older stones are rapidly repaired and, in 1999, money was allocated for the gradual cleaning of markers. The result is impressive. When driving into Achorn, the hillside literally sparkles with white stones.

Witness Rockland's ongoing history through Achorn Cemetery, and in doing so, please pay your respects to Arthur Dean at the Cremains Garden. Arthur was the superintendent for twenty-five years and had a special relationship with this cemetery, where he knew every lot by name. Perhaps it is his special spirit that imbues Achorn Cemetery with a quality of "tender-loving-care."

Rockland

GLEN COVE AND SEAVIEW CEMETERIES

Directions: From Route 1 in Rockland, north of downtown, look for the Samoset Resort Information Building on the corner of Route 1 and Waldo Avenue. Turn onto Waldo Avenue and follow the signs to Samoset Resort. The cemetery is immediately across from the entrance to the resort. Follow the street to the end of the cemetery for the oldest graves.

By all appearances the Glen Cove and Seaview cemeteries are one cemetery, but in actuality the Rockland Cemetery Association maintains the first three-quarters, and the town of Rockland maintains the last quarter, where the most of the oldest graves are found. I will refer to the cemeteries as Glen Cove Cemetery for the sake of simplicity.

There is more character in the stones at Glen Cove Cemetery than may at first appear.

My first impression of Glen Cove Cemetery was that it was too big, too boring, and too new. But further exploration was forced upon me when I realized that many of the stones were facing west, and I would have to wait several hours to take photographs. During that time I found many wonderful epitaphs and a number of monuments and headstones that deserved admiration. Though the cemetery was established in the early 1800s, most of the gravestones date from the mid-1800s to the present. You'll find a few slate markers, a zinc monument, an abundance of marble and granite stones, many impressive Victorian carvings and interesting family plots. The well-maintained grounds are crowded but park-like with a variety of shrubs and trees, and though it is close to the ocean, there is no view of the sea or of Glen Cove.

Glen Cove has several stones with exceptional drapery carvings, often in the form of parted fabric like stage curtains, revealing an open book. This carving signifies the passageway to heaven and the book represents the Bible. There are several in this style that are elaborately adorned with flowers and tassels, but Benjamin Brewster's 1849 marker is the most ornate. Drapery carvings became popular during the Victorian Era when the home was emphasized. On monuments, a draped urn was also popular and symbolized grief over earthly death.

Amanda M. Snow's 1855 inscription follows:

> She died to sin to woe to care,
> Yet for a moment felt the rod,
> Then springing on the viewless air,
> Spread her light wings and soared to
> God.

Approximately two thirds down from the contemporary graves and to the back is the full-body relief portrait of James F. Sears, who was surely loved by his fellow firefighters. The inscription follows:

> Who lost his life while
> gallantly performing his
> duty as a Hoseman of Dirigo
> Engine Co. No. 3 by the
> falling of a chimney at
> the burning of the Com
> mercial House, in Rock
> land, on the evening of
> Dec. 20, 1859. æ 20 y

The impressive monument to firefighter James Sears features a realistic carving of the deceased.

137

5 ms & 20 ds.
Erected to his memory by
Dirigo Engine Co. No. 3.

The Commercial House, where he died, was a popular hotel built in 1857.

The ship's anchor and cannons on this gravestone indicate the deceased's Naval service.

There are many veterans' stones throughout the cemetery, and several interesting Civil War markers close to the back road near the Sears' monument. Many veterans' stones were issued by the government, with varying sizes and amounts of information depending on the war. For example, during the Civil War the government provided inscribed wooden tablets for fallen soldiers. The short lifespan of these markers bought about a seven-year debate about what type of gravestone should be supplied. Finally, in 1873, polished marble stones with rounded tops that were four inches thick, ten inches wide, and twelve inches high were approved for Union soldiers. Confederate stones were not approved until 1906 and differ in that they have a pointed top and do not have the shield insignia of the Union markers. They are typically laid out as follows:

Rank, name and company number
Co. G
4th ME
Inf

A Civil War veteran's gravestone in the vicinity of the Sears' monument was purchased by his family and is inscribed:

Nathaniel C.
Son of Jona S.
& Melinda C. Stubbs.
of Co. A. 17. U.S. In-
fantry, died in An-
napolis. Md, Mar
19, 1865.
19, 1865. æ 21 yrs.
& 7 d's.
A victim of Rebel ill treatment
In Libby, (?).
(The inscription continues, but is no longer legible.)

The grave of Charles Holmes can be found near the center of the first drive that runs parallel to the road. Holmes died in 1863 at the age of 69, but lives on in Rockland's history. The War of 1812, and the years preceding it, devastated much of the coastline's shipping business. The ill-advised Embargo Act of 1807 forbade all foreign shipping in an attempt to stop the harassment of American ships by the British. The British seized cargo from ships and also "impressed," or forcibly took for the purpose of forced labor, thousands of seamen, claiming they were deserters from the British Navy. Many area men fought the British without officially joining the armed services as their lives were so tied to the sea. In 1813, Holmes was aboard the American privateer *Wasp* when it was captured. He spent eighteen months in England's Dartmoor Prison. At the end of the war he was released and indentured to Charles Spofford of Shore Village, as Rockland was called until 1850. Holmes had become friends with Spofford's brother in prison and from him gained the connection.

Childhood innocence became more and more idealized through the 19th century, and this was reflected in headstone and epitaph choices. Before the 1830s, children's graves were miniature versions of adults', but by the Victorian era there was a distinct difference in headstones. Those who could afford it chose a sculptural image such as a lamb, angel, or sleeping child, all symbolizing innocence. Less expensive stones were small, plain marbles carved with lambs, angels, flowers, or wilting buds. Glen Cove has one gravestone with an unusual carving of an angel with a baby on its back. Epitaphs were frequently sentimental in nature. Though there is no date on the precious epitaph that follows, it is probably from the late 1800s.

Little Elva
The dimpled hand,
the ringlet of gold,
Lie in a marble sleep;
I stretch my arms for
the clasp of old,
But the empty air
is Strangely cold,
And my vigil alone I keep.

The following Victorian epitaph offers the same sentimental love to departed parents:

• When grim death that
mighty monarch,
Tears our parents from us away
How our heart strings
seem disserved (sic)
And we almost hate to stay.

The Glen Cove Cemetery is a good place to observe the differences between marble and limestone, since limestone is more prevalent here. George Ulmer burned the first limestone in the late 1780s and for the next one hundred years it was of major importance to Rockland's economy. By 1828, Rockland had 160 lime kilns and thirty wharves dedicated to limestone shipping. In the 19th century it was considered to be the capital of limestone production. Limestone, or calcium carbonate, is very porous and dissolves easily. In Glen Cove Cemetery many markers are literally dissolving into the ground. The maintenance staff keeps up with repairs, so the easiest way to distinguish between marble and limestone is to note the stones that are being pieced back together with either braces or adhesives. If the stone is also porous with a very faded inscription, chances are it is limestone. Acid rain damages both marble and limestone, though limestone is more susceptible.

During the middle of the 19th century, cemeteries became tourist destinations complete with guidebooks and postcards (a trend I'm trying to revive). They were commonly viewed as meditative places where one could expect to learn valuable life lessons from the epitaphs and to be inspired by the accomplishments of others. Women were encouraged to expose their children to cemeteries to remind them of the shortness of life and acquaint them with death. I can imagine Glen Cove Cemetery developing in such an era, with its pastoral layout and impressive markers. It is still a place where people can find peace, calm, and learn valuable life lessons.

Vinalhaven

JOHN CARVER CEMETERY

Directions: From Route 1 in downtown Rockland, turn right into the Maine State Ferry Service. The ferry from Rockland to Vinalhaven is one hour and fifteen minutes. The cemetery is within walking distance of the ferry terminal. From the terminal, walk towards the village center and take a left onto High Street. The cemetery will be at the top of the hill on the right.

John Carver Cemetery slopes gently down to Carver Pond. Family plots terrace the hillside with granite curbing. Along the shore and the eastern boundary, wild flowers grow in abundance. Thankfully, the cemetery is barren of trees, leaving the view of the water interrupted only by the monuments of Vinalhaven's first families. The cemetery is a surprising sight on an island of this size. The noble granite monuments proudly populate a graveyard that would seem more at home in a prosperous and populous mainland community.

The cemetery owes its appeal to the granite industry that began in the 1820s and shaped Vinalhaven's history and culture. For one hundred years Vinalhaven was one of the busiest granite suppliers in the Northeast. Large numbers of experienced quarry workers were brought in from the British Isles and Scandinavian countries, and Italians were especially sought after as master craftsmen.

The 1870s marked the beginning of twenty years of unprecedented good fortune. During this period, Vinalhaven's granite was nationally renowned. Locals referred to this as the "government times" because federal contracts created a boomtown. The contracts called for granite for the War and Navy Department buildings, the base of the Brooklyn Bridge, and post offices in Cincinnati, Buffalo, Saint Louis, and Kansas City among others. Their most famous work was for the Custom House in New York City.

In the 1880s, the population peaked at 2,855 and gainful employment was available to all who desired it, including women who made fishing nets and horse nets for American Net and Twine. Secure incomes led to a vibrant community life. Social and cultural activities included skating parties, theater, music concerts, opera, costume parties, traveling troupes, medicine shows, and a number of men's and women's clubs. Vinalhaven was quite worldly thanks to their busy seaport, which exposed the island to people, ideas, and cultures from far outside Maine.

The cemetery was incorporated in 1871 by a board of trustees, several of whom were among the first settlers. The total cost of the land, including the granite fencing, was $1,726. Plots were sold for $5 to $40, and one plot was put aside for transient children because it was not deep enough for adults. Records indicate that Mrs. Rachel Smith was the first interment in 1845. There are many markers dating prior to 1871, though there is no clear record establishing whether the area had already been in use as a burial ground, the bodies were moved here, or the headstones were erected but the bodies were left on family property.

The monuments in John Carver Cemetery reflect the success of the early families. The names found here are a who's who of the first settlers: Arey, Carver, Coombs, Dyer, Ginn, Green, Hopkins, Smith, Pierce, and Roberts. The monuments stand as testimony to the lovely granite and the highly skilled craftspeople who created them. The carvings are topnotch, with details not usually seen on granite. By polishing the granite or leaving it rough, elaborate designs were fashioned. Several designs to watch for are the crown

The elaborate and ornate monuments of the John Carver Cemetery reflect the success of Vinalhaven's early families.

and cross, an armed soldier within a shield, the profile of a Civil War soldier shouldering his gun, and the U.S. Signal Corps emblem. Under most circumstances, lichen will grow only on unpolished rock, which creates the weird fuzzy effect found on some of the monuments. Also, notice the variety of granite colors that were found in the local quarries: brown, gray, salmon, and first-grade black. Many monuments incorporate two colors.

Cemeteries are not exempt from passing fashions, so there are also many imported marble stones. It is possible that local artisans carved the imports, though it has not been determined for certain. Most of the marble has held up well, and many of the stones remain spotless. The Hopkins family monument, found on the right when entering the cemetery, is exceptionally rich in details. Hopkins is spelled in twig letters and several border designs and motifs are used.

Towards the back, on the left, are two markers by Charles Athearn, who was a talented stone carver at Bodwell Granite Company and one of the men who carved eagles like the one keeping watch over Main Street in Vinalhaven. Athearn's family stone is a sculpture of a flat-topped cairn featuring a branch vase expertly carved from a single block of granite. Nearby, at the Wentworth family plot is a sculptured tree stump and branch.

While the Athearn monument appears to be a cairn of stones, it is actually carved from a single block of granite.

The Athearn memorials are unique, but even more unusual is an anvil in the Littlefield family plot, which can be found halfway through the cemetery in the center section. Not surprisingly, Charles Littlefield was a blacksmith whose tasks included crafting the metal rims for the large galamander wagons used to carry granite slabs. One is on display on the green across from the library.

An impressive amount of attention is paid to veterans in the cemetery. According to the 1870 obelisk on the town green, 169 men enlisted in the Civil War and 23 of them died. Emblems commemorating the G.A.R., or Grand Army of the Republic, and the "Ladies of the G.A.R." can be found on many graves, along with crisp flags. The G.A.R. was founded in 1866 for Union veterans of the Civil War. It was active in creating soldiers' homes, providing relief work, and pushing for pension legislation. At its peak membership in the 1890s, it was a formidable political force.

Note that two of the Carvers buried in the first plot on the left died in the Civil War. Other early veterans are from the War of 1812 and the Spanish-American War. The following veteran's inscription is from a monument with the ornate crown and cross, plus it also has an urn and drapery etching.

Herschel V. Young
U.S.N.
Died on Board
USS Castine
Feb. 12 1900
Age 18 Y'RS. 8 Mos.
Buried in
Bubbling Well
Cemetery
Shanghai China
Cuban War Veteran

Moses Webster has an understated monument halfway down on the left. He was a skilled granite cutter, an owner of the Bodwell Granite Company, a trustee of the cemetery, a selectman, a legislator and a senator. Moses descended from John Webster, who arrived in the Colonies in 1634. His former home is currently a bed-and-breakfast across from the green.

There are many good epitaphs here and most of the stones can be easily read. The most moving belong to the Lindsey family. Their three stones are three-quarters of the way down, in the center section, just in from the road on the left. The following is from a single stone, but be sure to read all the stones and even the back of one to get a full understanding of this family's story of loss.

The gravestones of the Lindsey family tell of tragedy and loss.

Betsey A.
died May 4, 1854
æ 16 yrs. 9 mos.
George H.
died Sept.19, 1847
æ 2 yrs. 5 mos.
Lucy Ann
died Sept. 1, 1836
æ 1 yr. 2 mos.
Children of Ephm. &
Sally Lindsey
They died in beauty as the
snow
On flowers dissolves away
They died in beauty as a star
Is lost at break of day.

The losses continued when the father and one son were lost in the same shipwreck, and then two more sons died in their twenties, one at sea. Sally Lindsey, the matriarch of the family, remarried and lived to be 88 years old, but chose to be buried with her first family. Her heart-wrenching epitaph states,

How many hopes lie buried here.

At first sight you may be fooled into thinking that all the John Carver Cemetery has to offer is its stately beauty. But it is a cemetery that reveals its riches slowly, demanding that you take the time to observe and reflect. Do that and you'll be rewarded with time well spent.

Also of Interest:

On your way to the cemetery you'll pass the **Vinalhaven Historical Society**, which features ongoing exhibits on many facets of the island's economic, social, and cultural life. "A Self-Guided Walking Tour of the Town of Vinalhaven and Its Granite Quarrying History," is a fun way to get acquainted with the area. The brochure is offered free of charge. They have a large number of photographs, records, and genealogical information and are willing to share. Open

June 12 through September 3, daily from 11:00 to 3:00. They are accessible year-round and can be reached via telephone, mail, or e-mail. P.O. Box 339, Vinalhaven, Maine 04863. Tel: (207) 863-4410. E-mail: *vhhissoc@midcoast.com*. Website: *www.midcoast.com/~vhhissoc*.

The island has thirty cemeteries, and the majority of them are small family lots. The most beautiful is the **Lane's Island Cemetery**. It is a small family burying ground located on preserve land and cradled by wildflowers and ocean.

The **Calderwood Cemetery** is one of the island's oldest and holds the graves of settlers who came in the 1760s, after the French and Indian Wars. A homemade videotape at the Vinalhaven Historical Society documents the cemetery stone by stone and the tragedy of Mary Calderwood and her ten children. Several of her children died in infancy. Mary and the remaining children died when she opened her home to several sailors who were sick with "ship's fever"—an earlier name for typhus. She soon died, along with all her children and the sailors. It was said that coffins could not be built fast enough, and the house was filled with bodies waiting for their burials.

GROVE CEMETERY

Directions: From Route 1 in Belfast, take the exit for Route 3, but do not get on Route 3. At the end of the exit, turn east onto Main Street. The cemetery is on the left.

Grove Cemetery is situated on a busy thoroughfare that leads to Belfast's scenic and historic waterfront. It is a large cemetery of twenty acres with nine thousand graves and still growing. In the old section, huge trees border the lanes, while new trees continue to be planted to beautify the grounds. The oldest stone is from 1799, though it is not original to the cemetery. In 1850, the First Church Cemetery was moved here. Old cemeteries were frequently moved as towns grew, and in Belfast the move was rather clumsy and some graves were lost or left behind. There is a "paupers' patch" that was originally in the center, but is now in the northeast corner.

Like many towns in northern Maine, Belfast was not settled until after 1763, when the Treaty of Paris was signed, effectively ending the French and Indian Wars. The first comers were Scotts-Irish farmers from New Hampshire, who purchased the land from Waldo's heirs. According to local legend, the settlement was named in 1768 when two men flipped a coin to decide whose hometown name would be used: Belfast, Ireland or Londonderry, New Hampshire. The man from Ireland won the day.

After the turn of the century, Belfast rapidly grew from a frontier town to a commercial hub. Belfast's residents were proud of their community and unusually proactive in its promotion. By 1820, Belfast was successfully marketed to businesses, migrants, and ship captains, creating a steady expansion. A new town hall was built with the expressed intention of luring the county seat from Castine, which when it occurred, contributed to the demise of Castine's golden era and helped extend Belfast's prosperity through the 19th century. The success of that era lives on today through the Greek Revival and Federal homes that line the streets and the brick buildings that form a waterfront business district.

Enter the cemetery through the wrought iron gates, and you will find yourself amid the graves of Belfast's most notable people. The Crosby's are considered one the town's most important families. William Crosby moved to Belfast from Massachusetts in 1802, after determining that the growing community held potential for a young attorney. His timing was excellent as there was more work in town than the one other lawyer could handle. His son, William G. Crosby, also an attorney, was elected governor of Maine and served three terms. He was busy throughout his life with state politics and authored the book, *Annals of Belfast for Half a Century*.

Another state governor buried here is Governor Hugh Johnston Anderson, who was elected in 1843 and served for three terms, plus two terms in Congress. He was considered to be very cultured, yet unpretentious, and his interests ran to literature, language, and history.

The large granite-slab stone, which lies flush to the ground, belongs to the Honorable John Wilson, 1777 to 1848. He was elected to Congress and served with Daniel Webster, who was his close friend. Wilson was a member of the "Lazy Club," which was a tongue-in-cheek collection of professional men who were prohibited from committing acts that took too much effort. Behind him are the graves of his son and his three grandchildren. All three grandchildren died in the Civil War.

Along the main road is the Johnson family plot with a large obelisk. Reverend Alfred Johnson is believed to have been the first burial in Grove Cemetery in 1837. His wife Sarah soon followed him in 1838. The Reverend only preached in Belfast for eight years before he resigned due to a pay dispute.

Alfred and Sarah's descendant, Anne Sarah J. Monroe, was a true heroine. Her husband, Doctor N.P. Monroe, was a surgeon for the 20th Maine Regiment, and she followed him to war in the service of the Sanitary Commission, where she worked in a military hospital at the front, caring for the sick and wounded. Her obituary states that she had "a natural disposition to do good," which is born out by her service in the war and by her activity in assisting fugitive slaves in the Underground Railroad.

Charles Bellows Hazeltine was the richest man in Belfast during his time. In 1849, when the gold rush sent thousands out West in search of their fortunes, Hazeltine used his creative business sense to earn his wealth without ever having to pan for gold: he supplied merchandise to the '49ers. He returned to Belfast at the age of twenty-six rich enough to retire. He continued to pursue a variety of enterprises, including shipping and the coasting trade between Belfast and Jacksonville, Florida. Perhaps he was one of the first snowbirds, as he wintered in Jacksonville. Hazeltine had the reputation of a warm, generous man who loved the outdoors. In fact, he is credited with introducing brush-shooting, bird hunting without the use of dogs, to Maine.

Also in the Hazeltine family plot is the grave of Patrick Henley, who was Charles' gardener for many years. Henley had a wife and children, though they are not buried with him.

Phineas Parkhurst Quimby's epitaph states:

> Greater love hath no man than this,
> that a man lay down his life for
> his friends.

The many followers of Doctor Quimby, as he was called later in life, believe that in 1866 he did lay down his life for others by exhausting himself through his spiritual-healing practice. Certainly Quimby is Grove's most fascinating resident. An Internet search revealed forty-seven pages of references, including a New Jersey church named after him and based on his teachings. People have been known to seek out his unassuming Belfast home to pay homage to his memory. Quimby and his followers believed that he had found the method Jesus had used to heal. Quimby is said to have healed 12,000 people by means that he could only explain by using a daguerreotype as a metaphor. In simplest terms, he received images of people's illnesses and the beliefs they held that had brought the illness about. By exposing people's faulty beliefs, which according to him were mostly brought on by medicine and religion, he imaged positive beliefs onto the person and cured their illness, thus, he believed, duplicating the faith healings of Jesus.

Quimby foreshadowed the mind-body alternative approach to healing in 1860 when he said, "I prophesy a time when men and women shall heal all diseases with the words of their mouths." He believed that seventy percent of illnesses were caused by wrong beliefs and that sickness was often determined by lifestyle and preconceived notions of illness.

In 1862, Mary Baker Eddy, the founder of Christian Science, was treated by Quimby and afterwards studied with him. According to the Quimby camp, Eddy was inspired by Quimby and based Christian Science on what she learned from him. In the late 19th century, Eddy became embroiled in controversy when it was claimed that she had Quimby's manuscripts and took much of her material from them. She vehemently denied the accusation. During her life, Eddy acknowledged that she was treated by Quimby, but experienced only temporary relieve from her symptoms. She broke with him because of his hostility towards religion and came to view him as only a mesmerist (called hypnotist today.) She claims that her inspiration for Christian Science came from a revelation and healing that she experienced after a serious accident in 1866 and is totally unrelated to her dealings with Quimby or to his healing methods.

The back of Frank Dickerson's handsome relief stone lists the numerous Civil War battles in which he fought, including Antietam and Brandy Station. He was badly wounded twice and became gravely ill from disease. Nearing death, Frank started home to Belfast while his father went to Boston to meet him. He died in his father's arms aboard a steamship in Boston Harbor. After three years in the Cavalry, he died in 1866 at the age of twenty-four. *Dearest Father: The Civil War Letters of Lt. Frank Dickerson, A Son of Belfast Maine*, by H. Draper Hunt, presents seventy-seven letters that Frank wrote to his widowed father, accompanied by an illuminating narrative.

The number of interesting carvings is limited, but there are several standouts. There are three angel statues that are beautifully expressed and are frequent models for students from the Maine Photographic Workshops, a very reputable photography school in Rockport. The oddest carving belongs to Jacob McDonald, who died in 1847. His stone has a relief carving of a hand with the forefinger pointing upwards, certainly nothing special—except that the hand has six fingers! Douglas Coffin, a Belfast resident whom I accompanied on the cemetery tour, is a craftsman who hand-cuts

One of three angel statues to be found in Grove Cemetery.

The exquisitely rendered angels are frequent models for photography students.

gravestones, an art that is seldom practiced anymore. He is mystified by the carving and explained that it would have been a simple mistake to rectify because the carver could have simply removed the last finger without compromising the hand. There are no clues in the inscription as to why there are six fingers, so it will remain a mystery.

Grove Cemetery has a noble ambience due to the headstones and family plots of Belfast's "movers and shakers." Adding to its dignity is the stone storage house formerly used to hold bodies during Maine's long winters, and a chapel that is being renovated. A wide time span is covered from the early headstones that were moved from the First Church, through the 19th century to the present. All in all, a very interesting cemetery.

Also of Interest:

Belfast's oldest graveyard is the **East Belfast Cemetery**. The land was set aside in 1769, and it is here that the earliest settlers rest in graves marked by fieldstones and slates or not marked at all. The burial ground is beautifully placed in a waterfront woodland setting. A lovely epitaph found marking the death of a mother and her four-day-old infant states, "Her babe is encircled in her right arm." It is located approximately 1 mile from the east end of the Memorial Bridge on Route 1 north. A stone church is almost directly across the street from the cemetery driveway, which is unmarked. A tall mailbox is just after the driveway.

Megan Pinette is the president of the Belfast Historical Society and the local cemetery expert. She gives an engaging tour of Grove Cemetery that brings Belfast's history alive. For more information, write Megan Pinette, 12 Allyn Street, Belfast, Maine 04915 or *www.mpinette@midcoast.com.*

The **Belfast Historical Society & Museum** is housed in an 1830s brick Federal-style building that was originally a store and home. The museum features the Percy Sanborn painting gallery, a maritime commerce exhibit, and revolving exhibits on Belfast's history. They have a collection of Belfast artifacts as well as postcards, photographs, maps, scrapbooks, books, and archives. 10 Market Street, Belfast. Tel: (207) 338-9229. E-mail: *belfastmus@yahoo.com.*

Part Three

DOWN EAST

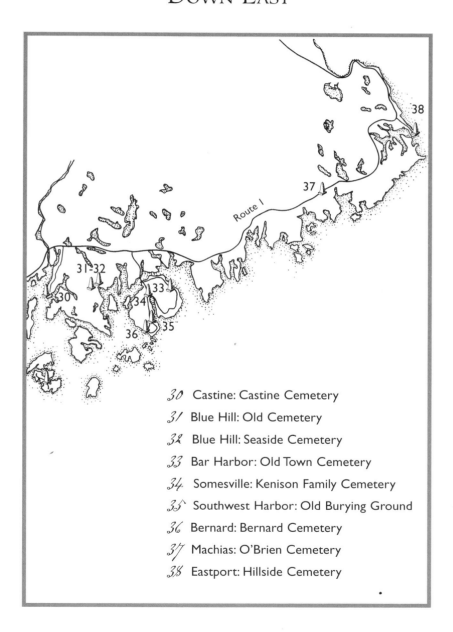

Castine

CASTINE CEMETERY

Directions: From Route 1 in Orland, take Route 175 south.
This will turn into Route 166 south. In Castine, Route 166
bears right, but continue straight onto State Street. At the
end of State Street, turn left onto Court Street. The cemetery
is the first left.

Welcome to Castine. Certainly it is one of New England's most beautiful town. Majestic elm trees miraculously escaped the blight and line the streets where clapboard houses are elegant reminders of Castine's golden years. Castine prospered throughout the trials of the 19th century due to its fortunate placement on the large, deep, protected harbor at the head of Penobscot Bay. Opportunities in commerce and transportation were plentiful, creating a vibrant economic, political, and social environment. The success held until the mighty shipping businesses of Castine failed to make the shift from sail to steam. By the 1870s, steamships dominated the commercial routes, and the great sailing vessels became a thing of the past. Ironically, the steamships brought to Castine its next industry—rusticators. The tourists had arrived.

Castine's valuable port led to its prolonged and intriguing military history. Starting in the 17th century, Castine has been occupied by the French, Dutch, and British at varying times. The last occupation was by the British in 1812. Castine is also home to America's most disastrous naval battle. The Penobscot Expedition of the Revolutionary War was marked by poor leadership and indecisiveness. The vastly outnumbered British were able to force the American fleet up the Penobscot River, where they scuttled their ships and walked back to Boston, with Lieutenant Colonel Paul Revere among their ranks.

The Castine Cemetery, with its views of the bay and pretty landscaping, is as visually captivating as the village. It is a cemetery of approximately twenty-five hundred gravestones that date from the 1790s to the present. A wide spectrum of grave markers is represented: slates, marbles, tombs, granite monuments, and some unique contemporary stones.

To find the oldest stones, take the second left from the entrance road. The two oldest graves are near the end of the lane, on the left, towards the center. The boulder with the brass plate is Castine's most fascinating grave and possibly the earliest burial in the cemetery. Lieutenant Charles Stewart was a British soldier stationed here during the Revolution. There is much speculation around his death. One story claims he fell in love with a local girl and killed himself when her affections were not returned, while another cites the possibility of a duel, though the former explanation is the most widely accepted. The tablet reads:

The oldest grave in Castine Cemetery is that of a British soldier stationed here during the Revolution. The cause of his death, however, has become lost to time.

In Memory of
Charles Stewart
the earliest Occupant
of this Mansion of the
Dead, a Native of Scotland
& 1st Lieut. Comm. of his
B.M. 74th Regt. of Foot,
or Argle Highlanders,
who died in this Town, while
it was in possession
of the enemy
March A.D. 1783
and was interred beneath
this Stone, æt about 40 y's.
This tablet was inserted
A.D. 1849

Stewart was the earliest recorded burial, but the earliest marker can be found directly in front of his. It states:

In Memory of
Thomas Fields Junr
son of Thomas &
Lucy Fields
who was drowned
before his Father's door
July 21st 1790
Aged 2 years & 3 days

Moving up the hill and to the right, look for the slate stones of the Mann family. Dr. Oliver Mann was Castine's first settled doctor and a Revolutionary War veteran. During the War of 1812, the British occupied his home while his family lived in the cellar. He was amicably described as a man who swore when he was angry, but was otherwise likable. At the age of seventy-six he caught a "severe catarrah," or cold, while going through wet grass to see a patient. Another trip out turned the cold to laryngitis and resulted in his demise.

The marble gravestone of Civil War casualty, Lt. Charles Little features a cross, sword, wreath, and drapery.

There are many splendid marble stones here, with one of my favorites belonging to Charles Little. It is carved with a pleasing ensemble of cross, sword, wreath, and drapery. His inscription reads:

Charles Little
Son of
Joseph L. and D. L.
Stevens
1st Lieut
14th Regiment Me. Vols.
Wounded Before
Port Hodson, Miss.
June 28,
and Died July 24, 1863
Aged 34 Years
If Need Be, I Will Lay
Down My Life
For the Cause of Freedom

In this town of veterans and sea captains it is an unexpected pleasure to find two teachers enjoying local fame. *Abigail and Sarah Hawes of Castine: Navigators & Educators*, by Mark E. Honey, tells the story of the sisters based on diaries left behind by Abigail. The Hawes sisters were very intelligent, but they were also blessed with characteristics common to those who are considered "gifted": motivation, curiosity, creativity, and a love of culture and life. The sisters complemented each other well, with Abigail being the romantic lover of poetry, history, and art, while practical Sarah excelled at math, logic, and chess. They broadened their horizons with frequent excursions to museums, libraries, and exhibits. In 1848, they left Castine to teach in several different states, but returned to the Hawes Academy that they are most remembered for. It offered a college preparatory curriculum that included Astronomy, Navigation, Arithmetic, Spelling, Science, History, Greek, French, Spanish, English, Literature, Penmanship, and Bookkeeping. Their stately granite monument can be found at the intersection of the entrance road and the third right. Abigail's epitaph is a testament to her individuality and her enthusiasm for life.

All the Bounding Universe is Alive.
There Are No Dead.

Close to the flagpole is the Tilden family plot. Captain Charles W. Tilden, a veteran from Maine's 72nd Regiment, escaped from Libby Prison in 1864. After the war, Tilden was a major backer of the schooner *Juliet Tilden*, which was named for his wife. In the fall of 1867, during a storm off the Magdalene Islands in the Gulf of Saint Lawrence, the *Juliet Tilden* was wrecked. Eighteen men and boys, some of whom are buried here, were lost, leaving behind eight widows and sixteen children.

Joshua Chamberlain, who is buried in Pine Grove Cemetery in Brunswick, is one of Maine's most prestigious heroes. He gallantly commanded the 20th Maine Infantry in decisive Civil War battles and went on to become the governor of Maine. His lesser-known brother, Thomas D. Chamberlain, who is buried here, was also in the 20th Maine and rose through the ranks on his own merit and skill to become Lieutenant Colonel of Company G. He fought courageously at Gettysburg and was among those engaged in the famous "bayonet battle" in the fight for Little Round Top. By war's end, Thomas had fought in twenty-five battles and skirmishes.

After the war, he struggled with deteriorating health and an inability to maintain a steady income. Both problems were either brought on or exacerbated by his overindulgence in alcohol. A bright spot in the post-war years came when he married his former sister-in-law, Delia, several years after the death of his brother, and her husband, John. Thomas' early death at age fifty-five is considered tragic as it appears that his alcoholism robbed him of reaching the potential in civilian life that had been so obvious during the war. He and Delia are buried downhill from the flagpole. His stone has an evergreen shrub and a solar-operated garden light provided by a visitor who believes she is the descendent of Thomas' illegitimate wartime offspring. Apparently several people have made that claim, though no proof has surfaced. His inscription reads:

> Thomas D. Chamberlain
> Died
> August 12, 1896
> Aged 55 years
> Lieut. Col. 20th Maine Vols.
> Brevet Col. U.S.U
> A faithful and distinguished
> soldier for his country.

Also of Civil War renown is Noah Brooks. His marble stone is close to the road, near the slate stones at the top of the hill. He was the Washington correspondent for the *Sacramento Union* when he became a close friend and political confidant to President Lincoln. Lincoln's assassination dashed his hope of becoming the President's private secretary. He later worked for the *New York Times*, the *New York Tribune*, and the *Newark Daily Advisor*, and authored two books on Lincoln.

The last tomb in the row on the hill belongs to Arthur Somers Roche, who penned thrillers and short stories. He was first published in the *Saturday Evening Post*, but it was his book *Loot* that brought him fame and fortune. He lived in Castine for six years as a struggling writer and returned as a visitor whenever possible.

In the newer section of the cemetery is the stone of Mary McCarthy, 1912 to 1989, who authored twenty-eight non-fiction and fiction books. She graduated from Vassar College, Phi Beta Kappa, in 1933. She had an extraordinary range of interests and wrote partially autobiographical novels, memoirs, historical reviews of arts and architecture, cultural criticisms, and political analysis.

Amazingly, this hidden cemetery in out-of-the-way Castine has the grave of another person of cultural note. Eileen Farrell, 1920 to 2002, was one of the leading soprano opera singers of her time. In 1962, she opened at the Metropolitan Opera House in New York City and gave a total of forty-five performances until her finale in 1966. Unlike many opera singers, Farrell successfully crossed over into pop music with her albums, *I've Got A Right to Sing the Blues* and *Here I Go Again*.

While exploring, be sure to travel to the newest section of the cemetery, where you will find some heartwarming contemporary stones. Technology has always dictated gravestone styles, and sandblasting techniques are moving us away from the plain granite blocks that dominated the 20th century to individualized stones that have stories to tell. A poignant example is near the back road where a lovingly tended grave, with a sandblasted nature scene, is patiently watched over by a statue of a dog.

Many contemporary graves feature very individualized motifs.

You'll find the Castine Cemetery to be in good condition, and thanks to the efforts of Brian Adams and his dedicated staff of volunteers, it will be steadily improving. Through the Wilson Museum, Adams is documenting and surveying the cemetery to create a database that will include all material from the markers and eventually genealogical information. Thankfully, they are also cleaning each of the stones as they move through the cemetery, and the difference is readily observable.

The residents of Castine would undoubtedly prefer that the town be excluded from all guidebooks so that they can keep this treasure to themselves. But like the rest of Castine, their cemetery is just too good to pass up.

Also of Interest:

The **Wilson Museum** has an eclectic array of offerings. It houses a large anthropological collection of tools and crafts from around the world. It also has a replica of a 1905 American kitchen and an operating blacksmith forge. Check their website for information about their ongoing cemetery documentation. Open May 27 through September 30. Tuesday through Saturday from 2:00 to 5:00. 107 Perkins Street, Castine. Tel: (207) 326-9247. Website: *www.wilson museum.org.*

The **Castine Historical Society** offers an interesting exhibit that brings to life Castine's rich history. Open July 1 through Labor Day. Tuesday through Saturday from 10:00 to 4:00, and Sunday from 12:00 to 4:00. Tel: (207) 326-4118.

"**A Walking Tour of Castine**," produced by the Castine Merchants Association is an informative brochure that brings you to all the highlights of Castine and easily familiarizes you with the town's history. The brochure is found free in most businesses.

Blue Hill

THE OLD CEMETERY

Directions: From Route 1 in Orland, take Route 15 south into Blue Hill. Turn right at the junction of Route 15 and Routes 15/176. Turn right onto Route 177. Look for the cemetery sign on your left.

The Old Cemetery in Blue Hill is in a landscape of boulders, ledge, and tiered earth; it's an unusual but dramatic choice for a burial ground and perfectly complements the historic stones and monuments. The prominent slate stones are easy to read, as is the marble that has fared better here than at Seaside Cemetery on the bay. You'll find seventy-three gravestones, including twenty-five Revolutionary War veterans, many original settlers, and lots of interesting epitaphs.

The cemetery was established in 1794, with the first and last internments occurring in 1800 and 1884. Originally a broad road led horses and carriages under an iron canopy into the cemetery. The geography of the cemetery proved difficult when a flash flood washed

More than a third of the graves at Blue Hill's Old Cemetery are those of Revolutionary War veterans.

away fifteen feet of cemetery in 1860. One casket was reburied, another had its end covered, and the surrounding picket fence was destroyed. Like many burial grounds, it suffered from years of neglect until it was reclaimed and recorded in 1962. Oral histories report that at the turn of the century there were many more markers, which can be confirmed by the disturbed unmarked ground.

Mehitable Witham is the first known burial, and her stone is to the far left from the entrance. The slate stone is in wonderful condition and is carved with an attractive folk-art urn.

One of the two earliest settlers of Blue Hill is buried here with his wife. Their great-granddaughter is responsible for the tablet that lies between their head- and footstones and commemorates him as an original founder of the town of Blue Hill.

Joseph Wood brought his family here a year after his arrival. He and his wife had six children, were married for seventy-two years, and both lived to ninety-three years old! In town history, the Woods are noted for entertaining the Revolutionary War colonel Rufus Putnam, who later settled Ohio. Wood's inscription reads:

> In Memory of
> Captain Joseph Wood
> Born Feb. 26, 1720
> Died June 20, 1813
> Aged 93 years
> He was the first our Forests tried
> Respected lived; lamented died
> Of seed, a numerous worthy train
> Survived his memory to sustain

Her inscription reads:

> In Memory of
> Mrs. Ruth Wood
> Wife of Capt Joseph Wood
> Born Dec. 3, 1721
> Died Apr. 6, 1814
> Aged 93 years
> Full three score and ten of Life
> She spent the chaste and loving wife
> Devoted, reserved, a neighbor kind
> Peaceful in days, in death resigned

Near the center of the cemetery is a sixteen-foot-tall obelisk that is the Fisher family monument. Parson Jonathan Fisher became Blue Hill's first settled minister in 1796. He was a brilliant Renaissance man of boundless energy and intellect. The short list of his talents includes: preacher, artist, author, teacher, carpenter, farmer, missionary, linguist, wood engraver, clock maker, record keeper, surveyor, and inventor. He graduated from Harvard Divinity School and filled his small house with nine of his own children and at least four or five young men who he educated for the ministry. As an ardent abolitionist he was involved in many political and missionary activities. Of his wife, little is said, but it is safe to presume that this remarkably busy man must have had a remarkably busy woman by his side.

Often in small towns the epitaphs lack variety due to a prevailing style stemming from the local carver or minister. In the Old Cemetery, the diverse epitaphs are poetic, religious, historic, or instructive. The exception to this is found by looking only at the children's epitaphs, which have a consistency in style and are unusually harsh for the period. In early Congregationalism, children were taught to fear death, and it was used as a tool to scare young ones into behaving. In the 18th and 19th centuries, general attitudes toward death softened, and death came to be viewed as a salvation and a reward, but here remnants of the old beliefs survive.

Ministers often wrote not only the funeral sermons, but also the headstone inscriptions. Perhaps Parson Fisher, who was known to be a conservative and zealous Congregationalist, wrote these epitaphs that are so similar in tone. The following examples sternly remind viewers that even children must fear the Grim Reaper.

Sally Prince Holt
Died Nov. 14, 1803
æ12
Nor youth sprightliness can save
From the all devouring grace

Peter Faulkner
Aged 4 yrs 4mo
Death is a debt to nature due
I've paid my debt so must you

Sarah Holt
Died Nov. 18, 1831

Aged 9
Children who read these lines begin
While young to fear the Lord
Believe in Christ; forsake your sin,
And reach a rich reward.

Here lies the bodies
of
Martha Herrick
who died Jan. 24, 1830
Aged 44 years and 1 month
and
Martha Herrick
who died Oct. 24, 1830
Aged 9 months and 14 days
Insatiable death will leave his prey
Nor youth nor age his mighty grip can stay.
The Mother falls beneath his power
And soon the infant's forced to cower.

This gravestone is adorned with a variation of the willow and urn symbol.

The Blue Hill Historical Society has published a beautifully done booklet entitled, *The Old Cemetery 1794*. It includes a map of the graveyard, inscriptions, and some biographical information on the deceased. If possible, purchase the booklet before your visit as it helps make for enjoyable exploration, but, even without it, this is a wonderful place to soak up the ambiance and delight in the history.

Also of Interest:
The Holt House is home to the Blue Hill Historical Society. It was built in 1815 and remains very close to its original form. Each room is gradually being decorated in the appropriate period. *The*

Old Cemetery 1794, along with other historical booklets, can be purchased here. Open July to September 15. Tuesday through Friday from
1:00 to 4:00, and Saturday from 9:00 to 12:00. Water Street, Blue Hill.

Parson Jonathan Fisher was truly a fascinating character, and a
visit to the **Parson Fisher House** is a testament to his talents and
indefatigable energy. Open from July 1 to September 15. Monday
through Saturday from 2:00 to 5:00. Routes 15/176, Blue Hill. Tel: (207)
374-2161.

*The epitaphs at historic Old Cemetery range from poetic and
religious to historic and instructive.*

Blue Hill

SEASIDE CEMETERY

Directions: From Route 1 in Orland, take Route 15 south into Blue Hill. Turn left onto Route 176. At the fork, bear right onto E.B. Hill Road. The cemetery is on the right.

Enter through Seaside Cemetery's exquisitely rusted wrought-iron gate to be greeted by a monochromatic vision of mottled and aged white marble. It is at once haunting and intimately beautiful. Look carefully into the bordering trees that drop to the sea below, and you'll find an inviting bench offering a view of Blue Hill across the bay. At the tip of the peninsula, tree limbs, ocean islands, and boats frame a Presbyterian cross. It couldn't be any prettier.

Seaside Cemetery is at once haunting and intimately beautiful.

Stones dating from 1833 to the present face parallel dirt roads that dissect the grounds into orderly sections. The older stones are in the center, with the contemporary markers along the edges. "Washington monument" obelisks are everywhere, but, thankfully, their monotony is overshadowed by many fine Victorian stones carved in the lush romantic style of the era. There are also two fine statues: Hinckley's woman holding a cross and the ornate Gothic Revival monument belonging to Asa Clough.

There are forty-two Civil War veterans buried in Seaside Cemetery. A local stonecutter, William Merrill Howard, carved the 1883 monument of a soldier near the front gate. He was experienced in carving decorative cornices and gargoyles, but this was his first figure. The local Grand Army of the Republic post commissioned the work at the cost of $1000. They were involved in the project right down to voting on whether or not the soldier should bear a goatee.

Down the third avenue, just past the tree that has literally grown around an iron fence post, are two interesting marble stones laid flat in a concrete bed. His states:

> To Die is to Gain
> Nehemiah Hinckley
> d. 1837 75 yrs
> He served in the Revolution as Colonel
> Smith's 6th Mass. Regt. From Feb. 17, 1781 to
> Dec. 31, 1782 when he was discharged at
> West Point and walked from there to
> Blue Hill

Hers states:

> Edith
> Wife of Nehemiah Hinckley
> D. 1863 97 yrs
> Old age is a crown of glory
> When it is found in the ways of righteousness.
> Edith Wood Hinckley was the Daughter
> of Joseph and Ruth Wood and was the
> Third White Child Born in Blue Hill

(See the Old Cemetery in Blue Hill for more information on the Woods.)

I favor epitaphs that show a conscious decision was made to reveal something about the deceased to the reader. In this same area is the following:

> Azor Candage

Died
Nov. 11, 1854
æ 63 yrs
Farewell conflicting hopes and fears
Where lights and shades alternately dwell;
How bright the unchanging morn appears.
Farewell inconstant world farewell.

In the center section moving down towards the water is an 1843 epitaph remembering the lives of an eighteen- and a twenty-one-year-old. It suggests what most people understand; the young are mourned more deeply than others because their potential is glimpsed but never fully realized.

We felt their worth yet scarcely knew
How pure a light their spirits shed;
Till they had faded from our view,
And they were numbered with the dead.

Noting euphemisms for death and pondering how epitaphs reflect a family's beliefs around death is a common pastime for cemetarians. The following epitaphs appear to illustrate the Stovers' ambiguity, as she is definitely dead, while he is definitely not, and both are definitely sleeping.

Alonzo P. Stover
Died
Dec.14, 1876
æ 64 yrs. 6 mos.
My Partner Kind, My Children Dear
I am Not Dead, But Sleeping Here
and as We Lived on Earth in Love
So May We Dwell in Heaven Above

Sarah
Wife of
Alonzo P. Stover
Died
Sept. 6, 1880
æ 67 Yrs. 10 Mos.
O' Let Us Think of All She Said

And All the Kind Advice She Gave
And Let Us Do It Now She's Dead
And Sleeping In Her Lonely Grave.

At the tip of the peninsula on the left are three flat markers backed by a low stone wall and four cedars. They belong to the popular songwriter, Ethelbert Nevin, his wife, and their daughter. Nevin is quite obscure now, but at the turn of the century he was very popular. In 1898, Nevin sold more than six million copies of "The Rosary." He and his wife adorned their stones with musical stanzas and the words, "And our souls at home with God."

On the right side near the end of the peninsula is a fascinating monument belonging to Captain Chambert Adams, who lived from 1839 to 1902. Adams was the president of the Montreal Free Thought Club and past president of the Canadian Secular Union. His monument is carved with an intriguing emblem and an extensive quote from Thomas Paine.

Several contemporary sand-blasted stones along the far left road are worth noting. The most engaging is a black granite stone with an engraving of the earth. A careful study of the globe reveals that white dots are embedded in different countries. We can only assume that they represent nations to which the deceased traveled.

Seaside Cemetery has an aristocratic, Old World charm, reminiscent of southern cemeteries. Elegant monuments and headstones are in perfect harmony with the beauty of the natural surroundings. It is definitely one of Maine's prettiest cemeteries.

At Seaside, elegant monuments are in harmony with the natural surroundings.

Also of Interest:

East of the Verona Bridge on Route 1 in Bucksport is the **Buck Cemetery**, the family burial ground of the town's founder, Colonel Jonathan Buck. On his large granite monument is the outline of a woman's leg and shoe. Legend says that before moving to Maine in 1762, Buck was responsible for executing a woman charged with witchcraft and the stain that appeared on the stone after his death is her curse. If the cemetery gate is locked, the stone is still visible from outside the fence.

There are many Victorian stones at Seaside, carved in the lush romantic style of the era.

Bar Harbor

OLD TOWN CEMETERY

Directions: From Route 1 in Ellsworth, follow Route 3 to Mount Desert Island and Bar Harbor. In Bar Harbor, turn left onto Mount Desert Street. The cemetery is between the Episcopal and Congregational churches.

The Old Town Cemetery in Bar Harbor is an organized, small, and tidy graveyard neatly divided by a pedestrian path. Nestled between Saint Savior's Episcopal and Bar Harbor Congregational churches, it is dominated by a large monument dedicated to "Eden's Sons who were the defenders of the Union." Bar Harbor, which was incorporated in 1796, was referred to as Eden until 1918. The headstones are predominantly from the mid-19th century and are marble or limestone with few exceptions. There is a consistency to the headstones that indicates one carver produced them, or they were mass-produced as that technology became available during in the mid-1800s.

Old Town Cemetery is nestled between Episcopal and Congregational churches.

The gravestones and monuments of the sea captains are very impressive. Captain Higgins's motif is a wreath of roses encircling a winged hourglass. His inscription reads:

Cap. Higgins lost at sea 1823
45 yrs
Father though the years have passed;
since thou was lost upon a
Distant shore. Still we remember thee.

Captain James Hamor's monument is a well-done relief of a ship tossed in a stormy sea. It is commonly believed that a sinking ship always signifies loss of the entire ship, while a sailing ship may mean death on board. Possibly he died during a storm at sea without the ship sinking.

Families don't often name the cause of death, so this touching memorial erected by the deceased's brother deserves notice.

Lucreatia (sic) K.
Dau. Of
Rev. Wm. S. & Priscilla
Douglas
was killed by falling from
cliffs on Newport Mt. Eden Me.
August 3, 1853
æ 12
Dead but not forgotten
Erected by her Brother
AH Douglas, in 1880

A unique carving appears on a small marble stone. It is a shield of stars and stripes topped by a star. Beneath the shield is a three-linked chain, which is the symbol of the Independent Order of the Odd Fellows.

Faith in a rewarding afterlife is revealed in this epitaph for a fifteen-year-old boy who passed on in 1877.

His home is on that blissful shore,
Where rests no shadow fall no strain
Where those thy meet shall part no more
And those long departed meet again

Despite the uniformity of stones, the Old Town Cemetery conveys a pleasant and dignified air.

Due to the uniformity of the stones, the Old Town Cemetery appears somewhat sterile. Nevertheless it conveys a dignified air, and the surroundings make it a pleasant place for browsing.

Also of Interest:
The cemeteries of Mount Desert Island and the nearby islands have been meticulously researched and documented by Thomas F. Vining in his book **Cemeteries of Cranberry Isles and the Towns of Mount Desert Island**. It lists the names and dates of gravestones found in more than one hundred cemeteries and gives precise directions on how to get to them. If you fall in love with this area, as so many do, you may want to purchase the book and set about exploring. It can be found at the Bar Harbor Historical Society, Mount Desert Historical Society, and Port in a Storm Bookstore.

Saint Saviour's Episcopal Church next to the Old Town Cemetery should not be missed. Points of interest are the lovely memorials lining the walls and the brass plaque in the center isle marking the burial spot of "Gouverneur Morris Ogden." Burials underneath churches were a common practice in Europe and in metropolitan areas of the United States, but were not common in Maine. The grave's proximity to the altar was traditionally determined by the importance of the deceased. The closer the burial was to the altar, the higher the status of the person. Though Ogden's grave is interesting, the best feature of Saint Saviour's is the breathtaking memorial stained-glass windows. Ten are original Tiffany's, but the thirty-two others are just as gorgeous. The windows' dates range from 1886 to 1992 and they employ a variety of techniques and styles.

175

KENISON FAMILY CEMETERY

Directions: From Route 1 in Ellsworth, follow Route 3 to Mount Desert Island. On the island, take Routes 102/198 south. In approximately 5, miles turn right onto Pretty Marsh Road. The cemetery will be on the left in 1.6 miles, just past Northern Neck Road. There is no sign, so look carefully for stone steps into the woods.

The personalized gate of the Kenison family cemetery.

Stone steps create a path through the woods to a unique family burial ground. A lovely handmade fence surrounds it, and the matching gate sports a large "K" with Kenison spelled out above; all this has been accomplished with slender tree branches. The ground inside the enclosure is mossy and springy with wildflowers and interesting undergrowth. The cemetery is groomed, but retains a natural look. Visiting the Kenison Family Cemetery is like going to someone's house for the first time. You observe the care that's been taken, admire the décor, and guess at the inner lives of those who reside there.

The cemetery contains close to twenty markers, including a large recent monument that lists sixteen Kenisons with their ages at death. The youngest died at only eight days and the oldest was eighty-nine. A number of the markers are wooden crosses, which I have frequently read about but hadn't encountered until now.

The family cemetery was a tradition for early rural settlers, and Maine is home to thousands of them. Many are on property no longer owned by the family and have been forgotten or neglected. Others were originally on farmland that has been reclaimed by the forests and their locations are lost. With the many lost burial grounds in mind, it is an honor to visit this one, which has been so lovingly preserved.

Though seldom seen elsewhere, several of the markers in the Kenison Cemetery are wooden crosses.

Southwest Harbor

OLD BURYING GROUND

Directions: From Route 1 in Ellsworth, follow Route 3 to Mount Desert Island. On the island, follow Routes 102/198 south to Southwest Harbor. In Southwest Harbor, turn left onto Clark Point Road. Turn left onto High Road. The burying ground is a short distance on the right.

The Old Burying Ground of Southwest Harbor was the first public cemetery on Mount Desert Island. Europeans had been on the island throughout the 1600s and 1700s, but a graveyard was not established until the 19th century. It is hard to imagine that this wooded and melancholy burial ground was once a cleared and sunny hill. The first minister of the Congregational Church, Reverend Ebenezer Eaton, donated the lot from his farmland. There are approximately forty gravestones, dating from 1830 to 1910, but most are from the mid-1800s. The majority of the stones record deaths that occurred before the age of thirty.

Southwest Harbor's Old Burying Ground was the first public cemetery on Mount Desert Island.

The burial ground has been cleared, but no visible effort has been made to straighten twisting and sinking stones or to repair those that have fallen or broken. There are several Civil War Veterans whose graves are marked with new flags, but the overall mood is one of neglect. The marble stones have not aged well, though many are still legible, and there are several slates in excellent condition.

As you enter, notice the row of stones on the right. The first fallen stone is Reverend Eaton's wife, Abigail H., who died in 1830. This is the earliest stone, though probably not the first burial. The reverend died while visiting their daughter in Sedgwick, and his body was never brought back.

Along this same side is the marker of David E. F. G. Hopkins. A look at his footstone reveals the inscription D.E.F.G.H.!

Through the center is a line of headstones that belong to Captain James Whitmore, his wife Rebecca, and four of their children. James and Rebecca lived to the ages of eighty-six and eighty-two respectively. They buried five of their children, three of them within six months. Joseph was a ship captain who traveled on several voyages, but died at home from consumption (tuberculosis) at the age of twenty-nine. John died at sixteen from a fever he contracted while working aboard a ship. Sarah died at twenty-seven, Hannah at seventeen, and Joanna at twenty-six. Joanna is the only child not buried here. Sarah's inscription reads:

It's difficult to imagine that the wooded and melancholy Old Burying Ground was once a sunny hilltop.

Sarah
wife of
Smith Robinson
Died
Nov. 2, 1850
æt. 27
dau. of James &
Rebeckah Whitman
The relics of deported worth,
Lie shrouded here in gloom
And here with aching hearts we mark,
Our own dear mother's tomb

There are several headstones marking deaths that occurred in the late 1850s, which could have been caused by the diphtheria spreading through the area.

The funeral for Seaman Robert Roberts was said to be an impressive military service.

In the far rear corner is the headstone of Robert Roberts, who was killed by a fall aboard ship. In *Southwest Harbor Traditions and Records*, by Mrs. Seth Thornton, the funeral is described as an impressive and polished military ceremony that nearly all the residents attended. His stone reads:

In memory of
Robert Roberts
Seaman U.S.A.
Born in Wales
U.S.S. Powhatan
Sept. 1 1872
Aged 28 years
rest in peace
Erected by his shipmates

Thornton also writes about oral histories where it was recalled that at least one other sailor and several strangers were brought in from ships and buried here, but there are no records or markers to substantiate it.

In 1831, Mount Auburn Cemetery in Cambridge, Massachusetts, was established, and soon cities all over the country were attempting to imitate its elegant landscaping and grand design. In direct contrast is this little graveyard, where the dead were buried with no particular concern for order and little thought given to the placement of family members. The cemeteries were begun within a year of each other, yet they were worlds apart. In this forlorn spot, with so many early dead, it is easy to grasp the harsh reality of a rural settler's life.

Bernard

BERNARD CEMETERY

Directions: From Route 1 in Ellsworth, follow Route 3 to Mount Desert Island. Follow Routes 102/198 south. Take Route 102, following the signs to Tremont. At the fork on Route 102, bear right. The cemetery will be on your right.

Bernard Cemetery is a small simple cemetery across from a pretty inlet and backed by a wide stream. The stones date from the late 19th century to the present. It is generally not a cemetery that would be of interest except for a bit of local lore associated with it.

A "heavenly crown" is said to be discernible on Elias Rich's gravestone.

The gravestone of interest is that of Elias Rich. It is the large marble marker in the center with metal braces along its sides. After Elias's death in 1867, markings emerged on his stone that showed a likeness to him. Next, what appeared to be a "heavenly crown" graced his head. This was remarkable to locals, who had few good memories of Elias and suffered from his ardent belief that he was to be well rewarded in the afterlife. A crown can still be discerned from the back, and with considerable effort, on the stone's front, but Rich's likeness has been obscured by additional markings.

From *New England Cemeteries: A Collector's Guide*, by Andrew Kull, I learned of this poem about the legend. It is by Holman Day and published in *Pine Tree Ballads* in 1902. The following is an excerpt:

Friends placed above Elias' grave a plain, white marble stone,
And months went by. Then all at once 'twas seen that there had grown
Upon the polished marble slab a shading that, 'twas said,
Took on a shape extremely like Elias' shaggy head.
Then soon above the shadowy brows a crown was slowly limned,
And though Aunt Rich scrubbed zealously the thing could not be dimmed.

Machias

O'BRIEN CEMETERY

Directions: From Route 1 in Machias, south of downtown, before the University of Maine and just before the bridge, turn onto Elm Street or Route 92. There is a parking lot at the electric substation for Bad Little Falls Park. Walk through the park to a path that leads up the hill to the cemetery.

For those traveling up coastal Route 1, Machias is the first look at what locals refer to as the "real Maine." Masses of tourists generally do not wander this far north, so gone are the stylish gift shops and bistros. Espresso is nowhere to be found. The charm of Machias lays in its authenticity. The bustle is not created by people from away, but by those who live and work in and around this hub for Down East Maine. Though remote and unknown to many, Machias is recognized by Revolutionary War buffs as the site where the first naval battle of the Revolution was fought and won, and it is Colonel Jeremiah O'Brien, a feisty warrior of this battle, who brings us to the O'Brien Cemetery.

Small, moody O'Brien Cemetery wears its neglect proudly.

184

The O'Brien Cemetery is the family burial ground of Morris and Mary O'Brien and their descendents. Morris and Mary arrived in the newly settled Machias in 1765 from Cork, Ireland, by way of Kittery and Scarborough. They established a sawmill and had nine children; Jeremiah was the most famous.

In 1775, the British military was in painful need of lumber to build barracks for the steadily increasing numbers of soldiers sent to suppress American rebellions. The British engaged the support of Ichabod Jones, agreeing to let him leave Boston to deliver food to Machias if he would guarantee that lumber and firewood be loaded onto the British ship *Margaretta*. The *Margaretta*, under the command of James Moore, accompanied Jones to Machias. After much debate, the townspeople voted to exchange the lumber for food supplies. Meanwhile, however, word of the battles at Lexington and Concord had reached Machias and a small group of determined men banned together to stop the British from receiving the lumber. Benjamin Foster took a leading role, since he was the only one with military experience—he fought in the Battle of Louisburg in 1745 and in the French and Indian War from 1756 to 1763. The other leader of note was Jeremiah O'Brien, who was joined by his five brothers.

The group managed to cripple the *Margaretta* with two small sloops. In an amazing display of courage, they stormed the ship with pitchforks, axes, and a few muskets. Captain Moore was mortally wounded, and the second in command, who was injured and overwhelmed, surrendered.

The adventures of Jeremiah and his brother John did not stop there. They continued their military careers at sea; Jeremiah commanded the *Machias Liberty* and John was the 1st Lieutenant aboard the *Diligent*. Both patrolled Massachusetts Bay and prevented supplies from getting to the British. Two years later, Jeremiah became a privateer, commanding his brother's vessel, *Hannibal*. He was captured by the British and sent to Mill Prison in England. The ever-courageous Jeremiah devised an escape plan in which he completely neglected his appearance and cleanliness. After a period of time he shaved, washed, dressed smartly, and walked right out of the prison. He later reported that he had stopped at the warden's house to enjoy a drink with the other gentlemen, and then boarded a ship for France. He returned to America in 1781 and commanded the brigantine *Hibernia*. In 1900, a torpedo boat was named after Jeremiah in honor of his gallant performance in the Revolution.

Jeremiah's gravestone is a simple slate carved with an urn. It should not be confused with his nephew's, the Honorable Jeremiah O'Brien, who was one of the first representatives sent to the United States Congress after Maine became a state in 1820. He served from 1823 to 1829. His son, also a Jeremiah, drowned at the age of nineteen when he was a senior at Bowdoin College.

The earliest stones are dated 1799 and 1805 and belong to Morris and Mary O'Brien respectively. In 1927, the cemetery was incorporated, and burials were restricted to their descendents. Since then there have been only two burials. There are approximately forty-five graves, with the oldest stones at the base of a fairly steep hill, and it is here that you will find the only carving that is not a willow and/or an urn. It is a serene feminine face surrounded by petals.

The oldest graves in O'Brien Cemetery are located at the base of the hill.

Most of the stones are unadorned and there are few epitaphs, but here are two of my favorites:

> Tears cannot restore her
> Therefore do I weep

And:

Death but entombs the body: Life the soul
Man dies to live, & lives to die no more

The Hannah Weston Chapter of the Daughters of the American Revolution has maintained the O'Brien Cemetery since 1975. This task is difficult. Because of vandals, the picket fence is gradually finding its way into the surrounding trees and spray paint adorns one of the stones. It is difficult for urban graveyards to escape abuse. But this small, moody burial ground overlooking the Machias River wears its neglect proudly, and I suspect the O'Brien's wouldn't have it any other way.

Also of Interest:

The only building in Eastern Maine with a Revolutionary War history is the **Burnham Tavern**, built in 1770, and preserved since 1910 by the Hannah Weston Chapter of the Daughters of the American Revolution. The tavern enjoys a rich history, which is revealed through the relics of the original residents, Job Burnham and Mary O'Brien, the daughter of Morris and Mary. The Burnham Tavern is where the plan to attack the *Margaretta* was plotted, and it also served as the hospital where the wounded British were nursed after the battle. The museum houses period documents, tools, clothing, weapons, and even the original tap. Open mid-June through Labor Day from 9:00 to 4:30, Monday through Friday. Winter months by appointment. Main Street, Machias. Tel: (207) 255-4432.

In 1998, the *Portland Press Herald* printed an article by Harriet H. Price that mentioned the struggle of Julian Johnson to get the State of Maine to replace the 400-foot wall marking the **Atusville Burial Ground** that it removed while widening the street. According to local history, the cemetery was a forgotten African-American burial ground. African Americans populated the Atusville section of Machias from the 1780s until the 1950s when one or two remained. Atusville's beginnings can be traced to London Atus, who arrived in Machias as a slave in 1771. Atus served in the Revolutionary War and used the money he earned to buy his freedom. He married a white woman and together they had many children, thereby beginning the Atusville community. The burial ground may finally be receiving the respect it deserves, as several University of Maine at Machias professors and their students have been diligently researching the African-American community, and the neglected graveyard has taken on special significance. The Atusville

Burial Ground is heavily mounded, but has no markers to establish who is buried there, though it could contain anywhere from six to twenty bodies. The archeology professor, Mike Kimball, is awaiting results from ground-penetrating radar tests to establish the boundaries of the cemetery and the number of bodies. Mike Kimball, Marcus LiBrizzi, an English professor, and history professor Kay Kimball (No relation to Mike.) are taking a multi-disciplinary approach to the research with the goal of reconstructing the history, stories, folklore, and culture of this forgotten community. They also want to re-establish town maintenance of the graveyard and purchase a monument. For further information they can be reached by e-mail at *mkimball@maine.edu.*

Eastport
HILLSIDE CEMETERY

Directions: From Route 1 in Perry, turn onto Route 190, which turns into Washington Avenue in Eastport. When passing through Pleasant Point be sure to follow the 35-mph speed limit to avoid a hefty fine. Take a left onto High Street. The cemetery is .3 mile on High Street.

Full of contrasts, Hillside Cemetery is a good representation of the town of Eastport.

Eastport holds a special place in my heart. It is a paradoxical island town that is as beautiful as it is distressed, doing battle with both the past and the future. This small town at the end of the earth should be totally safe, but it isn't. Glorious views that make the spirit soar and beautifully preserved period homes are juxtaposed with decaying buildings, unlit streets, and empty storefronts that speak of gloom and depression. Even so, I would go back to this enchanting town in an instant. Eastport's gifts are its wonderful history, brought alive through the remaining 19th-century architecture, a gorgeous and active port, and its genuinely friendly townspeople.

In the 19th century, Eastport was one of the country's busiest ports due to its twenty-five-foot tides and deep harbor—the deepest on the East Coast. Port-related businesses included foreign and domestic commerce, commercial fishing and packaging, and shipbuilding. The town was also home to many successful smugglers, whose chief product for profit was flour. By the 1880s, the population had swelled to nearly 6,000. (It is currently around 1,900.) Rich sea captains, ship builders, merchants, smugglers, and an established middle class accounted for the booming economy. The social life was vibrant: opera, theater, costume balls, and an indoor ice-skating rink that also served for roller-skating in the warmer months.

The Hillside Cemetery is the perfect representation of Eastport, as it, too, is full of contrasts. There are views of the bay and Canada beyond, but you have to look past a ring of rundown houses with hanging laundry and assorted cars in the yard. This large, stately cemetery tells tales of an illustrious past and claims former usage as a park, yet it is evident that keeping it well groomed is a challenging expense. In fact, it is only in recent history that the town starting mowing the entire cemetery instead of only those stones with perpetual care. Stones that face in every direction are saved from a sense of chaos by dirt roads that create an organized grid. Photographers take heart. You'll have sun on at least some of the stones most of the day.

The feeling of ordered disorder can be explained in the development of the cemetery. The town recognized the need for a new graveyard as early as 1814, when their seaside burial ground was facing such serious erosion that caskets were becoming exposed. But Eastport remained occupied by the British until 1818, and it was not until 1819 that the old graves were transferred. Initially, graves were dug with little concern for order. Then, in the 1830s, plots were organized, and in 1846 family plots were established, and bodies were re-interred when necessary. The earliest headstone is dated 1800, though it was probably carved at a later date. There are a few early-19th-century stones, but most are from later in the century, with a large number that are of high quality. The cemetery is still accepting burials and expanding its land holdings.

The two large tombs were probably built by masons and hold more than two hundred bodies. Notice the set-in stone that is marked 5828. A Masonic calendar perhaps? In front of the tombs are the headstones of two British soldiers, Walter St. John and Thomas Raymond.

Near the tombs is a reserved veterans' section that dates back to the Civil War, though there are more than six hundred veterans throughout the cemetery. There are twelve from the Revolutionary War, but not all are marked. Local historian Terry Holt is gradually straightening out records and ordering government stones whenever it is appropriate. One such stone reads:

Daniel Granger
Drummer
Col. Wadsworth Regt.
Revolutionary War
1762–1845

Granger enlisted at thirteen to replace his sick brother and re-enlisted three more times. A story of his bravery has survived. While on guard duty, a great creaking was heard that so frightened the soldier at the next post that he shot off his musket and fled. Young Granger held his post, not at all scared by the sound, which turned out to be cracking ice. He was in Saratoga in 1777, was engaged in battle at General Sullivan's defeat in Rhode Island, and was at West Point when Arnold turned traitor. It was often the case that young enlisted boys served as musicians.

Another government-issue stone belongs to Captain John Shackford, a local shipbuilder and Revolutionary War veteran with an amazing constitution. He completed Arnold's doomed march to Quebec, despite the lack of provisions that created a hellish experience of starvation and exposure. Most of his company was captured in Quebec, where they were held in chains and suffered from smallpox. Upon his release, he broke his promise to his captors that he would not engage in battle, and joined with Washington. When the British occupied Eastport in 1812, Shackford authoritatively told them they had permission to stay. He refused, however, to sign an oath of loyalty, which normally would have resulted in the loss of his property, but the British remembered and admired Shackford's Revolutionary War activities, so he kept his holdings.

One of several recognized war heroes to be found in Hillside Cemetery is Edward R. Bowman, who served in the Union Navy and received the Congressional Medal of Honor for bravery during the attempted capture of Fort Fisher in North Carolina. He served on the USS *Ticonderoga* where, despite severe wounds, he acted swiftly to lessen the impact of enemy fire upon the ship.

In the oldest section of the cemetery is a monument topped with a draped urn. It is the heaviest monument found here and belongs to Union General Henry Prince. Prince, born in 1811, graduated from West Point in 1835. He was first wounded during the Seminole Wars in 1836, and again during the Mexican War. In 1862, he was appointed

Brigadier General of Volunteers and was captured at Cedar Mountain, but upon his release continued to prove himself through the remainder of the war. At the age of eighty-one, Prince committed suicide in London, possibly because his old war wounds caused him so much pain.

In this section is a simple marble obelisk that serves as a memorial to Civil War veterans. It is the marker of Captain Thomas Paul Roach, but one side lists the men of Eastport who died in the war. The first two listed, Sgt. Corbett and JNO A. Gray, were both killed advancing colors at the same battle, Chancellor's Hill.

Someone who goes unrecognized in Maine but is famous to Texans is Theodore Lincoln Chadbourne, who was the first officer to die in the Battle of Resaca de la Palma during the Mexican War. Chadbourne has a Texas fort named after him.

Of local note is Jonathan Weston (1782–1834), who was the second lawyer to arrive in Eastport. He was well thought of and allowed to enter politics immediately, serving in many different positions throughout his life. In 1807, he bought a lumber mill that supplied wood for local housing and commerce, built a wharf, and handled the legal affairs of area businessmen. He built the Federal-style Weston House in 1810, where John Audubon stayed during his visits to the area. Today it is an elegant bed-and-breakfast reminding us of his fine taste and prosperity.

Many sea captains are buried here with markers that bear their tales of death at sea. Towards the center of the cemetery is a monument of a broken mast with a coiled rope and the relief of a sinking ship marking the 1867 death at sea of a family of four. The broken mast symbolizes a pillar of society that has been "broken" by death. The epitaph follows:

> How sad their fate midst ocean waves
> Where they all sunk to watery graves
> But in God's word sweet hope is given
> That we shall meet again in heaven.

The following is an unconventional epitaph that is carved on the hard granite found in Rockland area cemeteries:

> Elijah Lincoln
> 1827

My Elijah dear thy sleep is cold
Thy form with earth is laid
Thy spirit I do hope to see
In heavenly robes array'd
This cheering thought with magic power
H(???)ets from grief its poison sling
And in this dark and dreamy hour
Bring hope and healing in its wing.

The language used is unusual: "magic power," "dark and dreamy hour," and "hope and healing on its wing." They speak more to a mystical, spiritual response in contrast to the religious wording typical of the period.

The most unusual carving is also the oldest stone. It is found in the area of the main gate, back a row. It belongs to Joshua Bradford and his wife Mary, and has recently been cleaned and repaired. The wonderful Masonic carving depicts a winged Father Time holding the hair of a weeping woman who is leaning on a broken column and holding a willow branch. The spade, scythe, hourglass, and other Mason symbols are included in the design.

An elaborate Masonic carving adorns the gravestone of Joshua and Mary Bradford.

Headstones are particularly effective when the epitaph and the decorative carvings work together to create pleasing aesthetics and an emotional response. This quality is found in a modestly sized marble stone that is richly carved with an ecclesiastical border framing a winged hourglass from which a hand extends to hold an open scroll. Inscribed on the scroll is the epitaph:

In Memory of
Hannah Elizabeth

wife of
Joseph Hornell
who died
Oct 17th 1852
Aged 26 yr's 6 mos
The beautiful have banished
and return not.

Hannah Hornell's elaborate grave-stone is carved with a winged hour-glass and a hand holding a scroll, on which is written her epitaph.

Hillside Cemetery, like Eastport, has an irresistible charm that can only be experienced by taking the time to absorb the rich atmosphere and history. The wide variety of epitaphs and the lovely marble carvings are engrossing. Though remote, it is a worthwhile trip, where you'll be rewarded with panoramic views, kind people, and a fascinating cemetery.

Also of Interest:

Terry Holt has done exhaustive research on Hillside's inhabitants: Michiner built steamships, Treat was the first to can lobsters, Leavitt smuggled flour, Harrington was a privateer, Coolidge patrolled for the Revenue Cutter Service, and Abbie Davis MacNichols came to town as a single woman, opened a milliner's shop, and built a three-story brick building on Water Street. That was a very short list of his fascinating characters. He also has in-depth knowledge of veterans and of Eastport's fishing and shipping history. Fortunately for us, he enjoys giving cemetery tours. Tel. (207) 853-4674.

Stop by the **Peavey Memorial Library** for a copy of *The Eastport Walk-About*, an extensive and detailed self-guided tour of Eastport's history. The tour includes 77 sites, 31 of them found in the concentrated historic district along the waterfront. Water Street, Eastport. Tel: (207) 853-4021.

The **Waponaki Museum and Resource Center** has an impressive exhibit of photographs, native clothing, tools, and baskets that the Passamaquoddys are famous for making. The exhibit is free of charge. Route 190, Perry. Tel: (207) 853-4001.

The **Passamaquoddy Cemetery**, off Route 190, is interesting. It is both similar to and different from traditional Euro-American cemeteries. I was struck by the numerous crosses and angels, and also by the heightened color. Often a boundary of colorfully painted rocks encircles the marker, and the marker itself may be brightly painted. Besides the interesting cultural comparison, the view of the bay is stunning. Exact directions to the cemetery can be obtained from the Waponaki Museum at the main entrance to the village.

Quick Guide

* special , ** very special, *** incredibly special

SOUTHERN MAINE

Kittery Point: Old Parish Burying Ground ***
- ◆ Mid-size cemetery with views of the Piscataqua River. Interesting nooks.
- ◆ Robert Browning epitaph. Large number of historically significant stones.
- ◆ Dates from the mid-1700s to the present.
- ◆ Historic 1730 meetinghouse.

South Berwick: Oldsfield Cemetery ***
- ◆ Mid-size cemetery. Serene woodland setting on a large pond.
- ◆ Large number of 18th-century stones. Interesting carvings and epitaphs.
- ◆ Dates from the early 1700s to the 1930s.

York Village: York Village Burying Ground ***
- ◆ Traditional village cemetery with more than 150 graves. Surrounded by historic buildings.
- ◆ Joseph Lamson portrait gravestone. Historically significant stones and setting.
- ◆ Dates from 1705 to the mid-1800s.
- ◆ Historic 1747 meetinghouse.

Alfred: The Brothers of Christian Instruction at Shaker Hill **
- ◆ Two cemeteries on retreat center grounds with pond, lake, trails, woodland chapel, and some Shaker architecture.
- ◆ Granite Shaker monument with six original stones remaining. The Brothers' Catholic Cemetery has identical, multiple crosses.
- ◆ Dates through the 1900s with exception of the six 19th-century Shaker slates.

Scarborough: Black Point Cemetery *
- ◆ Large, park-like cemetery on a busy street.
- ◆ Several Joseph Sikes gravestones.
- ◆ Dates from mid-1700s to present.

Portland: Western Cemetery **
- ◆ Large urban cemetery, heavily vandalized.
- ◆ "Old Catholic Ground" and a memorial to the Great Hunger erected by the AOH.
- ◆ Dates from 1829 to 1888, with only select burials after.

Portland: Eastern Cemetery ***
- ◆ Large six-acre urban cemetery. Disheveled, overcrowded, littered, fascinating.
- ◆ Abundant variety. Naval heroes, veterans, matching graves of commanders on opposite sides during the War of 1812.
- ◆ Dates from 1700 to the late 1900s.

Yarmouth: Old Ledge Cemetery **
- ◆ Mid-size cemetery with pastoral scenes and a view of the bay.
- ◆ Several Noah Pratt Jr. gravestones. Attractive monuments and marbles, though epitaphs are difficult to read.
- ◆ Dates from 1770 to the present.

Yarmouth: Pioneers Cemetery **
- ◆ Tiny burial ground one hundred yards from Ledges Cemetery.
- ◆ Twenty-four graves of Yarmouth's first settlers. Also called Indian Fighters Cemetery. All slates carved with winged death heads.
- ◆ Dates from 1731 to 1774.

Yarmouth: Baptist Cemetery *
- ◆ Quintessential New England church burial ground.
- ◆ Gravestones and monuments predominately from 1800s. Many easily legible epitaphs.
- ◆ Dates from 1796 to the present.
- ◆ Historic 1796 meetinghouse.

Freeport: Woodlawn Cemetery **
- ◆ Mid-size cemetery with a unique setting. Park-like and groomed through center—rough and tumble around the edges.
- ◆ Wide variety of old and new stones and monuments that are side by side. Paupers' area.
- ◆ Dates from the early 1800s to the present.

Freeport: Mast Landing Cemetery **
- ◆ Small cemetery in a semi-rural area surrounded by original stone wall. Historic houses nearby.
- ◆ Several Noah Pratt Jr. gravestones. Impressive headstones of prominent Freeport settlers.

◆ Dates from 1784 to the mid-1800s.

Freeport: Ward Free Will Baptist Cemetery *
- ◆ Small cemetery on a busy street overlooking bucolic fields.
- ◆ Interesting zinc monument. Many eas-to-read religious epitaphs.
- ◆ Dates from the mid-1800s to the early 1900s.

Freeport: Pote Cemetery *
- ◆ Small, hard-to-find cemetery with graves scattered through pine forest and a modern memorial garden.
- ◆ Graves of the prominent Pote family along with one contemporary headstone.
- ◆ Dates from late 1700s to mid-1880s, with one 1995 grave.

New Gloucester: Pineland Cemetery – Malaga Island **
- ◆ On the grounds of the former Pineland Hospital and Training Ground.
- ◆ Site of graves of black, white, and mixed-race residents of Malaga Island and of unclaimed residents of Pineland Hospital.
- ◆ Identical 20th-century stones.

Brunswick: Pine Grove Cemetery **
- ◆ Mid-sized traditional cemetery.
- ◆ Burial place of Joshua Chamberlain. Many noteworthy headstones and monuments.
- ◆ Dates from 1801 to 1979.

Harpswell Center: Old Common Cemetery ***
- ◆ Small church burial ground.
- ◆ Newly cleaned stones with interesting variety of carvers and many religious epitaphs.
- ◆ Dates from the mid-1700s to 1900.
- ◆ Historic 1757 meetinghouse.

Arrowsic: New Town Cemetery **
- ◆ Small, remote, woodland cemetery.
- ◆ Well-carved and handsome 19th-century slates and marbles.
- ◆ Dates from mid 1700s with a small number of 20th-century graves.

MID-COAST

Wiscasset: Ancient Cemetery ***
- ◆ Historic village burial ground with views of the Sheepscot River.

- Lengthy "virtue epitaphs" abound. Unconventional carvings.
- Dates from 1739 to the late 1800s.

Sheepscot: Sheepscot Cemetery **
- Mid-sized cemetery with beautiful, park-like grounds overlooking the head of the bay.
- Numerous Victorian stones in good condition.
- Dates from the mid-1800s to the present.

New Harbor: Fort William Henry Cemetery ***
- Small, historic cemetery overlooking the Pemiquid River; close to Fort William Henry.
- Several Joseph Sikes gravestones. Impressive headstones carved from imported Welsh slate.
- Dates from 1734 to the present.

Waldoboro: German Protestant Cemetery ***
- Large meetinghouse cemetery on an attractive hillside.
- Mostly marble headstones, obelisks, and monuments with interesting carvings and epitaphs.
- Dates from the late 1700s to the present.
- Historic 1772 meetinghouse.

Warren: Old Settlers' Cemetery **
- Small, secluded, woodland cemetery found at the end of a quarter-mile trail.
- Variety of both impressive and humble old stones in varying degrees of deterioration.
- Dates from the late 1700s to the early 1800s, with a 1913 monument dedicated to the town's first settlers.

Monhegan Island: Monhegan Cemetery **
- Small cemetery with spectacular views of the ocean, village, and Manana Island.
- Modest headstones with varying degrees of legibility.
- Dates from 1784 to the present.

Rockland: Tolman Cemetery **
- Small, well-maintained, hilltop cemetery with views of rolling fields and wooded hills.
- Revolutionary War veterans, unique granite and death-head carvings.
- Dates from the late 1700s to the mid-1800s.

Rockland: Achorn Cemetery **
- ◆ Very large cemetery with beautiful views of Camden Hills.
- ◆ Interesting monuments, rich history, many Victorian carvings and epitaphs.
- ◆ Dates from the mid-19th century to the present.

Rockland: Glencove Cemetery **
- ◆ Mid-sized cemetery with formal layout and park-like grounds.
- ◆ Many noteworthy monuments, obelisks, and Victorian head- stones.
- ◆ Dates from the mid-1800s to the present.

Vinalhaven Island: John Carver Cemetery **
- ◆ Mid-sized hillside cemetery at the water's edge.
- ◆ Impressive granite monuments from Vinalhaven's quarries. Athearn's carvings are of particular interest.
- ◆ Dates from 1845 to the present.

Belfast: Grove Cemetery **
- ◆ Large landscaped cemetery on a busy thoroughfare.
- ◆ Beautiful angel statues and unique six-fingered carving.
- ◆ Dates from 1799 to the present.

DOWN EAST

Castine: Castine Cemetery **
- ◆ Large traditional cemetery with water views.
- ◆ Numerous Victorian carvings, unique marker for a British sol- dier, many notable people and some interesting contemporary stones.
- ◆ Dates from 1783 to the present.

Blue Hill: The Old Cemetery ***
- ◆ Small, hilly burial ground with jutting ledge, shaded by many trees.
- ◆ The graves of Blue Hill's early founders. Interesting stones in good condition. Excellent guide to the cemetery is available at the Blue Hill Historical Society.
- ◆ Dates from 1794 to the mid-1800s.

Blue Hill: Seaside Cemetery ***
- ◆ Large, formal cemetery with stunning water views on three sides.

- Formal monuments and sculptures, aristocratic headstones, creative epitaphs, and some interesting contemporary stones.
- Dates from the mid-1800s to the present.

Bar Harbor: Old Town Cemetery **
- Quaint village cemetery nestled between two churches.
- Mostly uniform marble stones. Large Civil War monument and several Civil War veterans.
- Dates throughout 1800s.

Somesville: Kenison Cemetery **
- Family cemetery on a wooded lot enclosed by a cleverly designed handmade fence.
- Wooden crosses, traditional headstones, and a large granite block listing family members.
- Dates from the mid-1800s to the present.

Southwest Harbor: Old Burying Ground **
- Small woodland cemetery close to Southwest Harbor center.
- Noteworthy seaman's gravestone, Civil War veterans. Stones have varying degree of legibility.
- Dates from the mid- to late 1800s.

Bernard: Bernard Cemetery *
- Small, plain cemetery across from an inlet, with stream winding around it.
- Elias Rich's 1867 gravestone is the source of local legend.
- Dates from the late 1800s to the present.

Machias: O'Brien Cemetery **
- In a populated urban neighborhood, but in a wooded area overlooking the Machias River.
- Local heroes and veterans from the Revolutionary War. Early local and state politicians. One carved image and very few epitaphs.
- Dates from 1799 to the mid-1800s.

Eastport: Hillside Cemetery ***
- Large, traditional cemetery with views of Eastport's harbor.
- Many monuments, obelisks, interesting epitaphs, and notable people.
- Dates from 1800 to the present.

Glossary of Terms, Symbols, and Abbreviations

THE SYMBOLIC MEANINGS OF CARVINGS

Grave carvings are open to multiple interpretations, as are most symbols, that derive their meanings from the era, region, culture, spirituality, and individual associations. The following serves as a guide to the most commonly accepted meanings for grave carvings.

Acorn:	Strength, life, maturity.
Altar with an open book:	Free Mason. Meetings are opened with a Volume of Sacred Law, usually a Bible, on a table symbolizing an altar.
Anchor:	Hope, occupation at sea.
Angel:	God's messenger, divine guidance. Innocence when used on children's graves.
Angel with a sword:	Justice.
Archway:	Entry to the afterlife.
Arrow:	Death. Colonists may have associated arrows with death from Native American attacks.
Birds in flight:	Flight of the soul.
Book:	Word of God, Bible, wisdom.
Breasts:	Divine nourishment for the soul.
Celtic Cross:	Christian cross associated with Ireland. The circle signifies eternity. The knots bind the soul to the world, and the plaits signify the universe's loom.
Chain links:	Three links signify the Independent Order of Odd Fellows, IOOF. Also accompanied by FLT for friendship, love, and truth.
Clouds:	Transition to heaven, home of the divine.

Cloud with emerging hand:	God calling the soul to the afterlife.
Coffin:	Death of the flesh.
Columns:	Entrance to the afterlife.
Column obelisk:	Complete full life, pillar of the community.
Column broken:	Life cut short, loss of head of family.
Compass, set square, G:	Free Mason emblem. The compass symbolizes good spiritual life, self-control, and keeping boundaries; the set square signifies things of the earth, such as home; the G is for geometry, which reveals the glory of God.
Cross:	Faith, Christianity.
Cross with a crown:	Faith in eternal life, sovereignty of Christ.
Crown:	Eternal life, victorious soul. Biblical references include the crown of glory, life, and righteousness.
Cup:	Communion.
Dove:	Peace, purity of the soul, Christian devotion, Holy Spirit descending.
Drapery:	Parted fabric is a passageway to heaven. Drapery became popular during Victorian era, signifying the comforts of home.
Eye:	All-seeing, all-knowing God.
Father Time:	Inevitability of death. The Grim Reaper.
Finger pointing up:	The soul has gone to heaven.
Finger pointing down:	God calling the soul to heaven.
Flower:	Beauty and briefness of life.
Flower bouquet:	Grief, condolences.
Flower bud:	Young life unblossomed.
Flower with a broken stem:	Life cut short.
Gavel:	Free Mason symbol for self-control and discipline.
Grapes:	Communion, blood of Christ.
Grape vines:	Symbolism for Christ saying, "I am the true vine and ye are the branches."

Gourds:	Passing away of earthly things.
Handshake:	God's welcome to heaven, farewell to material life. If one hand is masculine and one feminine, it means marriage.
Hands praying:	Piety.
Heart:	Love, spiritual bliss, devotion. In Colonial symbolism it represents the soul in bliss, in Victorian it indicates romantic love.
Heart, cross, anchor:	Love, faith, and hope.
Horns:	Resurrection.
Hourglass:	Passage of time.
Hourglass with wings:	Swift passage of time.
I H S:	An abbreviated spelling of Jesus in Greek that has become a symbol for Jesus. On Celtic crosses it can signify "In His Service."
I N R I:	Latin initials for "King of the Jews."
Ivy:	Remembering friendship, fidelity.
Lamb:	God's children, Christ, redeemer. Innocence when on a child's marker.
Lily:	Resurrection, purity, Virgin Mary.
Moon:	Rebirth, mother, the feminine.
Oak leaves:	Maturity at death.
Oak tree:	Immortality, strong faith, endurance.
Obelisk:	Eternal life, connection between heaven and earth. In the original Egyptian symbolism the obelisk stood for the phallus of the earth god Geb as he united with the sky goddess Nut.
Palms:	Resurrection, victory over death.
Rose:	Love, beauty, motherhood.
Scallop shell:	Resurrection, birth, pilgrimage.
Scythe:	Divine harvest, life cut short.
Sheaf of wheat:	Harvested after a full life, abundant life, final harvest.

Scroll:	Scriptures, law.
Ship:	Occupation at sea.
Ship sailing:	Death on board.
Ship sinking:	Death in a shipwreck.
Ship in a storm:	Death at sea or during a storm.
Skeleton:	Death, mortal remains. Common usage began during the plague of the Middle Ages.
Skull with crossbones:	Mortal remains.
Snake swallowing its tail:	Eternity.
Spinning wheel & 13 stars:	National Society Daughters of the American Revolution, NSDAR.
Star:	Divine guidance, birth, Christ.
Star with 5 rounded tips:	Grand Army of the Republic, GAR.
Star with 6 points:	Star of David. Emblem of Jewish faith.
Sun:	Life, God.
Sun rising:	Resurrection, glory of new life.
Sun setting:	Death.
Temple:	Free Mason symbol for King Solomon's Temple in the Holy Land.
Thistles:	Remembrance, usually Scottish.
Torch:	Divine guidance.
Torch upside-down:	Extinguished life.
Tree:	Creation, faith, wisdom. The Tree of Life, which has been used since ancient times and is associated with creation and the origins of humanity.
Stump, branch, or fallen tree:	Life cut short.
Urn:	Death of the flesh.
Urn with wreath/drapery:	Mourning.
Vines:	Christ, church members.
Wheat:	Body of Christ.
Willow branches:	Free Mason symbol for grief. They are

	carried at Mason funerals.
Willow tree:	Earthly sorrow. Inspired by Psalm 137:1-2, "By the rivers of Babylon, there we sat down, yea we wept, when we remembered Zion. We hanged our harps upon the willows in the midst thereof."
Willow and urn:	Earthly grief over mortal remains.
Winged cherub or soul:	Soul's flight to heaven.
Winged death head:	Mortal remains of the dead joined with the wings that take the soul to heaven.
Winged globe:	The globe symbolizes the earth and creation; the wings are God over all creation.
Woman mourning:	Statues popular in the 19th century. May have derived from the Greek myth of Niobe; a mother forever mourning her children who were killed by the gods.
With a child:	Charity.
With an anchor:	Hope.
With a cross or Bible:	Faith.
Wreath:	Mourning, victory in death, eternity.

TERMINOLOGY

Aetatis, Æ, Ê, æt, Êt:	Latin for age.
Ancient burial ground:	In Maine state law, any private burial ground established before 1880.
Cenotaph:	An empty grave with marker erected in memory of the deceased.
Columbarium:	A structure found in cemeteries to hold cremated remains.
Consort:	Term found on early gravestones meaning the wife was survived by her husband. An example is, "Mary consort of John."
Consumption:	Tuberculosis.
Crypt:	A large underground vault for bodies.

Epitaph:	A message inscribed on a gravestone. In the Colonial period they were written mostly by ministers or taken from the Bible. As the 19th century progressed and people became more educated, verses from poems or songs were used. Stone carvers also kept a collection to chose from.
Exhume:	To remove the body from the grave.
Footstone:	A small stone used to mark the end of the grave. Sometimes they were plain, but usually they were inscribed with the name or initials of the deceased.
Fugit hora:	"The hour flies" in Latin.
Headstone:	An upright marker, usually rectangular.
Memento mori:	"Remember death" in Latin.
Obelisk:	A tall narrow monument such as the Washington Monument. They originated in Egypt and became popular memorials in the 19th century.
Re-interred:	Reburied.
Relict:	A term meaning the deceased woman was a widow at the time of her death. An example is, " Josephine relict of Samuel."
Requiescant in Pace:	"Rest in peace" in Latin.
Sarcophagus:	A stone coffin.
Sepulcher:	A tomb or grave.
Slab stone:	A large flat marker laid flush to the earth on a bed of pebbles.
Table stone:	A flat marker raised off the ground by four, six, or eight legs.
Tempus erat:	"Time was" or "time is gone" in Latin.
Tomb:	A grave marked by a raised base of brick or cut stone topped by a stone slab. Also, a large house-like structure designed to hold multiple bodies either above or below ground.

Tympanum:	The high center arch on headstones.
White bronze or zinc:	Monuments that were produced from 1880 to 1920 by the foundry industry, which was attempting to expand into the memorial business. The hollow zinc monuments were less expensive than the bronze that they were designed to imitate.

ABBREVIATIONS

AF&AM:	Ancient Free and Accepted Masons
AOH:	Ancient Order of Hibernians
BPOE:	Benevolent and Protective Order of the Elks
DAR:	Daughters of the American Revolution
F&AM:	Free and Accepted Masons
FLT:	Friendship, Love, Trust. Found on Odd Fellows' gravestones.
GAR:	Grand Army of the Republic
IOOF:	Independent Order of the Odd Fellows
K of C:	Knights of Columbus
K of P:	Knights of Pythias
KT:	Knights Templar
NSDAR:	National Society Daughters of the American Revolution
SAR:	Sons of the American Revolution
USA:	United States Army
USAF:	United States Air Force
USMC:	United States Marine Corps
USN:	United States Navy
VDM:	Verbi dei minister, minister of the word of God
VFW:	Veterans of Foreign Wars
WOW:	Woodmen of the World or Women of Woodcraft

Tips for Photographing Gravestones

RECOMMENDED EQUIPMENT

- Bug spray! The mosquito is jokingly referred to as Maine's state bird.

- Grass clippers to trim grass and weeds from the headstone's base.

- A soft-bristle nylon brush for cleaning and brushing away old clippings. Natural-bristle brushes are not recommended because the bristles could become lodged in the stone and promote growths. Do not clean chipping, cracked, or unstable stones.

- A spray bottle with water for cleaning. Do not use soap, vinegar, bleach, or any chemical cleansers as they will damage stones.

- Rags for cleaning.

- Gum erasers or wooden popsicle sticks for removing lichen. The lichen should be soaked in water, and then gently removed with the eraser or stick. Stubborn growths should be left to the professionals.

- A large mirror to reflect the sun onto the stone for photographs. Photographer's reflectors work well also, and are not as bulky.

- A TTL flash unit with TTL-dedicated cable, which allows the flash to be held at an angle to the stone, creating more depth.

- A tripod for flexibility. Slower film can be used for a finer grain; a smaller aperture can be used when increased depth of field is desired; a slower shutter speed can be used to increase details; and photographs can be taken in decreased light, such as at sunrise or sunset.

Helpful Hints

The most basic advice that can be given about photographing gravestones is that the pictures must be taken when you are eye level to the stone. Often that means lying down on the cold wet grass—something to consider when choosing an outfit for the day. Photographs taken from a standing position with the camera angled down onto the marker distort the stone and make the inscriptions difficult to read.

Before snapping the picture, remember to check out the surroundings. Does the grass need to be trimmed to reveal the entire stone? Are there dried grass clippings stuck to the stone? Are there weeds or fallen branches that will detract from the picture? If there is a flag from a veteran's grave flapping in the wind, it will show up as a blur unless you use a fast shutter speed. Lichen can be beautiful or a distraction. See the equipment list for removing it. Bird droppings must be cleaned away, though sometimes they stain or there are so many it's best to choose a different stone!

It is a good idea to write down the inscriptions and a description of the stones you photograph, especially if the pictures are for genealogical purposes. Bad camera days occur when the flash washes out the picture, the exposure is wrong, or there is no film in the camera. It happens.

Generally, people are buried in cemeteries facing either the rising or the setting sun. Most of the cemeteries on this tour have headstones that face west, making afternoon sun the best for photographs. There are also a number of graveyards where people were buried haphazardly, with no concern for east or west. Obviously, if the day is overcast, it is not going to matter, and some people prefer overcast days because of the lack of shadows. If you arrive too early or too late and must shoot into the sun, then use a flash to lighten the stone. A flash will work best when it is hand held at an angle to the stone, using a TTL cable. Using flash directly on a stone has a tendency to flatten the image and on granite can even result in a reflection. A mirror or photographer's reflector can also be used to lighten the stone. A flash is helpful in the woods when light is limited or dappled.

The best time of day to shoot depends on your goals. For sharp images of the inscription, the best time is 11:00 to 1:00, depending on the direction the stone is facing. The light coming from a high angle creates a depth in the inscriptions that shows up well in photographs. It works great on slate headstones, but can cause harsh shadows on ornate Victorian carvings. If pretty pictures are your goal, then the best time is the beginning and end of the day. Shadows soften, colors are warm, and the sky takes on rich hues. The best way to get a sharp inscription image at this time of day is to take the picture of the stone at an angle instead of from the front. At any time of day, water sprayed onto the stone will sometimes bring out the inscription.

The type of film to use is up to individual taste. I use 50 or 100 ISO color slide film and 100 or 400 ISO black-and-white negative film. Genealogists and historians prefer black and white for the clearest image of the carving and inscription. From an artistic viewpoint, you need a darkroom or a professional lab for black-and-white pictures to be printed with the correct contrast. I started shooting only black-and-white and now shoot color slide almost exclusively. You should experiment to find what type of film brings you the most satisfying images.

Grave Rubbings

Early burial grounds are our country's open-air museums, and the gravestones are the artworks. A well-carved gravestone is aesthetically pleasing, creative, evokes emotion, tells a story, and conveys information about a distinct time, place, and culture. Grave rubbing is a popular hobby where an image of the original art is captured on paper or cloth.

To get started you will need:

- ◆ Aqaba brand rubbing paper, butcher paper, mulberry paper, or rice paper.
- ◆ Genealogists recommend non-fusible medium to heavyweight interfacing fabric found in fabric stores instead of paper.
- ◆ Lumberman's crayon, rubbing wax, or jumbo crayons. Do not use ink or markers.
- ◆ Masking tape is the only acceptable adhesive, as others leave residue on the stone.
- ◆ Stone-cleaning materials from the list provided in Tips for Photographers.

Some cemeteries, however, have banned grave rubbing because of the potential for damage to the stones. Check with the cemetery superintendent, town clerk, or historical society before proceeding.

Do not make rubbings on stones that are flaking, crumbling, cracking, weak, or unstable on their bases. If a stone sounds hollow when it is tapped, then it is not suitable. Gently clean the stone using only water, a soft-bristle nylon brush, and rags. Do not struggle to remove small impurities. You may damage the stone, and they may add character to your rubbing.

Any stone can be rubbed, but slate stones are the easiest to work on and tend to produce the best results. Stones with a high relief or that are deeply engraved should be avoided as they will tear the paper. Rough stones or stones with a lot of lichen will not result in good rubbings.

Cover the entire surface of the stone with the paper or fabric, fold it around to the back and then use masking tape to secure the top and sides. Rub the crayon or wax over the entire surface of the stone. Try to go in one direction and work small sections at a time. Repeat the process until you've achieved the desired degree of darkness.

When you are finished, remove the tape from the stone, and be sure to clean up after yourself.

Gravestone-rubbing kits that contain all the equipment you need can be purchased. Beware of kits that use ink, because it will permanently stain the stones. The Maine Old Cemetery Association (MOCA) and Gravestone Artwear sell kits with grave-safe products. MOCA is a non-profit organization dedicated to locating, documenting, and preserving Maine's old cemeteries (*www.rootsweb.com/~memoca/moca.htm*).

For grave rubbing kits contact:
Maine Old Cemetery Association
David Clark
127 Cobbossee Avenue
Gardiner, Maine 04345-9050
(207) 582-7373

Gravestone Artwear silk-screens their gravestone rubbings onto T-shirts and elegant velvet garments and accessories. They carry an array of interesting products and artwork related to gravestones. Kits may be purchased at the retail store or by contacting them at:
Gravestone Artwear
PO Box 141
York Harbor, Maine 03911-0141
1-800-564-4310 or *www.gravestoneartwear.com*
Their retail store is located at 207 York Street in York Village.

Native American Graves
PROTECTION AND REPATRIATION ACT

When I first started this project, I had hoped to include Native American burial grounds as part of the tour. While trying to verify locations with Native American organizations or individuals, I was met with shoulder shrugs or silence. Finally, I was told what should have been obvious from the start—Native Americans did not want me to publicize their burial grounds' locations because for hundreds of years their remains have been exhumed and put into museums as cultural artifacts.

The clash of values between Native Americans and European settlers extended to beliefs about human remains. Europeans arrived without a strong sense of reverence for the body after death. In Europe, the church and government held responsibility for interments. Burials occurred in church graveyards, or for the prestigious, under church floors. Floors were often raised to accommodate the ever-growing number of bodies, and, after a period of time, old bones were removed to make room for the newly deceased. The remains were sent to ossuaries that were created for that purpose. Municipal burials were either in a family plot that was rented for six to twenty years or in massive trenches where layer upon layer of the dead were disposed of. In Paris, as in other cities, fear of disease emanating from the graveyards and trenches brought about a movement to move burials away from urban areas. This resulted in the establishment of Pere Lachaise, considered the first modern cemetery and the inspiration for Mount Auburn Cemetery in Cambridge, Massachusetts. Pere Lachaise offered perpetual care, which strongly influenced American cemeteries, but the tradition of renting family plots continued in Europe. Family plots are still rented, though now the time span may be as long as one hundred years. After payment lapses, the bones are removed and the plot is resold.

In the United States, our concern about preserving cemeteries is fairly recent. It was not until the 20th century that laws were established to protect graves. Prior to that, removing entire cemeteries for the sake of development was considered acceptable. Grave robbing had a long tradition throughout Europe, and in America it reached its peak during the 19th century, when remains were stolen for science and medical schools. Cemeteries were frequently abandoned and neglected.

Native Americans had a wide variety of death rituals and not all tribes buried their dead, but of those that did, the grave was sacred and not to be disturbed. Unfortunately, the United States did not honor those beliefs. For years, skeletons and grave objects were removed for placement in museums as archeological finds or cultural curiosities. Thousands of remains were collected and put into museums, including some from 19th-century battles. The lack of regard for human remains shown by those of European descent was, and is still, shocking to Native Americans.

In 1990, the Native American Graves Protection and Repatriation Act (NAGPRA) was enacted to address past injustices and prevent further violations. NAGPRA is a federal law requiring federally funded institutions to inventory their human remains and grave-related objects to determine if they are culturally affiliated with modern tribes. Museums were given five years to complete the task and make the remains available to the appropriate tribe. The law makes it illegal to buy or sell grave objects or remains. It also establishes that any remains found on federal or tribal lands after the enactment of the law belong to the lineal descendants, the tribe, the tribe whose land the grave was on, or the tribe that inhabited the land at the time of discovery.

As of 2002, a new Maine state law states that funerary objects and human remains found during federally funded archeological work and that can be affiliated with a modern tribe are subject to NAGPRA. But, if native remains are one thousand years old or more recent, and they can be associated with a tribe, then they are returned through the Maine Native American committee that deals with repatriation issues.

NAGPRA is not a perfect solution as there are complications to the law that make it cumbersome to both Native Americans and archeologists. Archeologists are long past digging up graves for museum exhibits, but they do believe that the scientific community has the right to study ancient remains. Presently, NAGPRA acts as a workable compromise between Native Americans and archeologists, though in the coming years it will be challenged in court, refined, and hopefully improved to everyone's satisfaction.